THE ENIGMA
OF GENDER

THE ENIGMA
OF GENDER

WHY IDENTITY IS
NEITHER INDIVIDUAL
NOR ESSENTIAL

HANS-GEORG MOELLER

Columbia University Press   *New York*

Columbia University Press
Publishers Since 1893
New York   Chichester, West Sussex
cup.columbia.edu

Cataloging-in-Publication Data is available from the Library of Congress.

ISBN 9780231221276 (hardback)
ISBN 9780231221283 (trade paperback)
ISBN 9780231563642 (epub)
ISBN 9780231565974 (PDF)

LCCN 2025035496

∞

Cover design: Milenda Nan Ok Lee
Cover art: 1981 Rustic Studio kan/Shutterstock

GPSR Authorized Representative: Easy Access System Europe,
Mustamäe tee 50, 10621 Tallinn, Estonia, gpsr.requests@easproject.com

CONTENTS

ACKNOWLEDGMENTS

After the long and somewhat winding path of completing the manuscript of this short book, some heartfelt thanks to the role mates, soulmates, and scroll mates who helped it along are in order. First, I wish to thank Wendy Lochner, my editor at Columbia University Press, for her most valuable and unwavering support and corrective advice. Without her professional competence and trust, this book could not have been published. Jorge Ponseti's proficient counsel and our extended discussions provided crucial inspiration and guidance. Rory O'Neill not only straightened out my English but also offered lots of thoughtful feedback and suggestions for changes and clarifications. Chan Lok Lam meticulously formatted the manuscript to make it submissible, and Nicholas Frankovich carefully edited it. Although Paul D'Ambrosio has not been a coauthor this time around, our previous collaborations on *Genuine Pretending* and *You and Your Profile* serve as the conceptual grounding for the present theoretical effort. Chiang Hio Fai on our YouTube channel *Carefree Wandering* produced several videos on (trans)gender identity that are thematically related to this book. I greatly appreciate the many constructive responses by viewers of this channel and readers of my books (especially Jared

Morningstar's essay on Medium, some suggestions by Clara S. Santana, and the coining of the term "scroll mates" by Charlie Abbott). Flemming Hansen and Fa kindly allowed me to use part of their interview for illustrating a point about (trans)gender identity in Asian contexts. I learned a lot from informal conversations with Marton Radkai, Markus Heidingsfelder, Inbal Shamir, and Andrea Martinez about gender, identity, and politics. An earlier draft of this book was written in Belgrade. There, the friendship and kindness of Milos Rancić, Žarko Aleksić, Uroš Krčadinac, Natasha Schmelz, and Milan Urošević has been precious. I express my gratitude to the University of Macau for supporting my research with a sabbatical and two generous grants: the Multi-Year Research Grant MYRG2022-00037-FAH on "Identity and Gender: From Role to Profile," and a grant from the 2024 Excellence Publication Scheme of the Institute of Advanced Studies in Humanities and Social Sciences (IAS).

THE ENIGMA
OF GENDER

INTRODUCTION

TOWARD A BETTER NARRATIVE ABOUT GENDER

During the process of writing this book, Wendy Lochner, editor at Columbia University Press, suggested I listen to a conversation between the journalists Lydia Polgreen and Masha Gessen on *The Ezra Klein Show*.[1] The title given on YouTube to the recording of the conversation summarizes the main point Gessen tries to get across: "We Need Better Narratives About Gender." The purpose of the present book is to work toward that goal.

If there is a need for better narratives about gender—and I think there is—we first need some clarity about what's wrong with the present ones. In the conversation with Polgreen, Gessen addresses a number of flaws that, to me, indicate three major and closely interconnected "epistemic obstacles"—that is, three problematic beliefs about gender identity—stemming from a Western philosophical and theological heritage. These obstacles need to be overcome to arrive at better narratives about gender. All three are tied to the *enigma of the gendered self*.

The first problematic belief is that gender identity is inherently *individual*.

At one point in the dialogue, Polgreen reflects on her experience of growing up as a biracial kid in the United States. She says that as a child she did not think of herself in racial terms and became aware of this "identity" only when confronted with a racist slur at the age of ten. This leads her to question the "nature of identity and the idea that there is some sort of sovereign self that you can anchor yourself to." Polgreen's doubts about the existence of an "immutable" racial self prompt Gessen, who is nonbinary, to problematize gender identity. Gessen responds: "Well that's another problem with the whole 'born in the wrong body' discourse. . . . I've always felt, and after a certain time was able to put words to it, that gender is something that happens between me and other people. It doesn't actually happen inside my body. It's what people see, what I want them to see, what I feel when they see one thing and not the other thing. All of that is my gender." Polgreen and Gessen realize that racial and gender identity are not unique traits of a person emanating from somewhere deep down in themselves. Instead, our perception of our racial and gender identity—a self-perception virtually everyone develops when growing up—emerges and takes shape in our interactions with others. And yet, our present-day narratives, rooted in philosophical-religious-linguistic traditions, suggest that others ultimately do not matter in questions of identity because true identity—including racial and gender identity—is to be found only in the "sovereign self that you can anchor yourself to."

At the very end of the conversation, Gessen recommends a book to the listeners: Miquel Missé's *The Myth of the Wrong Body*.[2] Missé is a Spanish sociologist and transgender activist. The book describes, on the one hand, his political and personal struggles.

On the other hand, in close relation to these struggles, it expounds a profound critique of the individualist concept of gender identity.

The myth of the wrong body bothers Missé, and he sets out to debunk it. It goes along with the belief that gender identity comes from "within." This belief informs what Missé calls a "cliché metaphor" in current transgender discourses: the claim that "if a trans person had been born on a desert island they'd still want to have surgery regardless."[3] Missé rejects this claim and points out the "extremely individualist" tendencies in Western neoliberal societies that the desert island scenario betrays.[4] It suggests that gender identity is inherent in a singular, sovereign self—even if no one else is present, a person's inner gender identity will eventually come to the fore in an imagined complete solitude. And, if this gender identity happens to be trans, a person will inevitably long for gender-affirming procedures. In Missé's opinion, however, "trans people born on a desert island wouldn't be trans: our gender expression would not be associated with any fixed gender identity and less still to a concrete social corporality."[5]

Missé conducts an alternative thought experiment: "If we were to leave a newborn baby on a desert island, with no other humans, to be cared for by a pack of wolves, and we returned to visit after fifteen years, when we asked them if they were a boy or a girl, their most likely response would be to bite us. . . . They wouldn't identify with other boys or girls, they would most likely identify with wolves."[6] Missé's point is not to deny that "feeling like a man or a woman" is "a specific subjective experience";[7] it certainly is; we all have such inner feelings. What he intends to highlight is that this feeling does not emanate from an elusive inner self irrespective of circumstances but rather that it's a "collective experience as well."[8] In reality, we grow up not on desert islands but alongside other humans. When growing up, we eventually "feel like a man or a woman"—and what that feels like is inevitably influenced by how we interact with one another in a gendered way. A feral child might well develop certain behavioral or emotional traits that scientists can classify as gender-typically "feminine" or "masculine," but the child could not *identify as* a man or a woman because they wouldn't even know these words. The child would have to learn from others what it *means* to be a girl or a boy. No one can *feel like* a boy or a girl if there are no other boys or girls around.

Echoing Masha Gessen's formulation that "gender is something that happens between me and other people," Missé affirms "the importance of the group and the community,"[9] that "social pressures condition us," that "what other people think affects us," and that "we might not be as original as we imagine."[10] The experiences of Polgreen, Gessen, Missé, and many other people with a "nonconforming" gender identity suggest that *gender identity— that is, a gendered sense of self—does not come about through a mysterious discovery of an inherent, individual, and gendered core self; instead, it is relational.*

The second epistemic obstacle preventing the rise of better narratives about gender is ontological. The premise of a gendered self tends to imply not only that gender identity is individual but also that it is *essential*.

Throughout *The Myth of the Wrong Body*, Missé argues against a current narrative about transgender that suggests that "trans people have a mismatch between their gender identity and their body because of an error in their biological development."[11] This narrative rests on a premise that, as Missé assumes, a "majority of people" share: namely, that gender is not "something someone simply identifies with, but something that someone *is*."[12] By emphasizing the word "is" here, Missé indicates the ontological belief that gender identity is a central aspect of an individual's true "being" rather than a psychological feeling, a social category, or a combination of both. This ontological approach to gender has created, as Missé says, the "monster of gender essentialism."[13]

Gender essentialism is expressed in the popular formula that a transgender person's self is "trapped in the wrong body—i.e., in a body with a different sex. This expression reflects a body–mind dualism related to the history of Western philosophy and theology: "gender identity" is ascribed to the immaterial, spiritual, and essential self, distinct from the material, organic, and inessential body it inhabits. This highly problematic dualism in turn gives rise to, in Missé's words, "a twentieth-century Western concept which assumes that if a person identifies as the 'opposite' gender to the one they were assigned at birth they have to change their body to match."[14] The implicit logic of this assumption is that a person's gendered self is in their consciousness and that, in order for the person to be fully and coherently themselves, their bodily sex has to correspond to the mind's gender. If there's an incongruity between the two, the mind must take the lead and the body must follow and, if necessary, be forced to fit the mind. The mind must, by its own sovereign will, impose a transformative regime onto the body so that it correctly manifests who this person *is*.

The ontological prejudice that gender identity is "something that someone *is*" brings about a third epistemological obstacle plaguing current gender narratives: *the normative expectation that a person ought, or ought to be empowered, to get their identity right.* Almost inevitably, any "is" implies an "ought."

Summarizing the flaws of current (Western) gender narratives, Gessen says to Polgreen: "Well, then, the problem is that we assign such disproportionate importance to both sexuality and gender. And so, if they are so important, so central to our identities, then how could they be accidental, how could they be chosen, how could they be mutable? We need them to be cores of who we are, and for that we have to invent all sorts of narratives about how they were always there." Our gender metaphysics, the idea that gender defines each individual's *being*, leads us to regard gender and sex with the utmost seriousness. Once sex and gender are regarded as the "cores of who we are," there is little to no room for contingency.

Therefore, our narratives about gender have always had a moralistic dimension: If people truly *are* men or women, they also ought to be *truly* manly or womanly. Accordingly, traditional societies formulated narratives to specify respective roles for women and men. More often than not, these roles were hierarchically organized and typically (although not always) reflected patriarchal orders. And even today, Miquel Missé says, we are "telling kids that there should be a natural concordance between the body, gender identity, and gender expression."[15] (This formulation, by the way, once more shows how we tend to infer a normative demand—"there should be"—from the ontological claim that something *is* "natural.") Gender narratives are often not merely descriptive; they tend to promote behavioral, psychological, and physical gender role (or profile) models that can exert an enormous ethical pressure or, in Missé's words, "symbolic violence."[16]

The symbolic violence of normative expectations to get one's gender right did not end with the demise of traditional societies. It extends, Missé claims, to our times. He criticizes, in particular, a capitalist cosmetic industry that has "learned how to monetize trans people's need for sexual reassignment, mainly women, by creating an expensive catalogue of bodily modifications that go very, very far beyond what could be considered any form of treatment. . . . If you want to be a woman you will need a pinch of this, a splash of that, and a large dollop of that over there."[17] In today's context, the pursuit of gender conformity is, as Missé demonstrates with some poignant examples, often paradoxically dressed in the language of authenticity. According to him, the "dominant narrative" of "trans empowerment" is the "conquest" of the body: it must be "bent to a person's will,"[18] resulting in a "cult of the individual's ability to transform" the body.[19] The conquest of the body, Missé says, is "associated with the values" of "authenticity, courage, perseverance, success." These values express a contemporary gender ethics, particularly when applied to transgender people whose transitioning process is celebrated as making "their body match the gender they identify with."[20]

Writing *The Myth of the Wrong Body*, Missé says, was "part of an almost therapeutic process of recovering my body, *reconquering* it through love."[21] To achieve this reconquest, he set out on a journey of "learning to accept [his] body," with or without modifications, simply to "live a better life."[22] During this process, he distanced himself from what he calls the "identitarianism" implicit in some gender narratives.[23]

Strong doses of normativity in identity narratives, including the narrative of today, make it difficult to accept the contingencies of selfhood. This is especially the case with regard to sexual and gender identity because, as Masha Gessen said, we assign such "disproportionate importance" to them. But there is, after all, an alternative. Gessen suggests, "What if we just agree to be playful and have fun with the one life each of us is given?"

Based on their own experiences with gender nonconformity, Miquel Missé and Masha Gessen express a deep frustration with the individualist, essentialist, and normative components of current gender narratives. Both realize that the *quest for becoming who you really are* is not the solution to the identity problem but, to the contrary, is its very origin. Eventually, both shift their approach to a *quest of being comfortable with whoever you happen to be*. Such a therapeutic, playful approach to identity and gender was already taken a few thousand years ago in philosophical Daoism.

A core intention of the present book is to show that no other philosophical resource is better equipped than Daoism to deal with the three epistemological obstacles that prevent us from arriving at better narratives about gender. Daoism does not share the premise of an individual and essential self. Instead, it understands identity as relational and contingent. What is more, by understanding that human selfhood is "genuinely pretended," Daoism has as its main concern not to get identity right, but to be at ease with oneself and others.

IDENTITY TECHNOLOGIES

If gender identity is indeed relational and contingent rather than individual and essential, we need to ask: Which relations condition gender identity? And how do they change over time?

Another intention of this book is to show that these questions—how do different types of social relations shape different notions of gender identity, and how did notions of gender identity evolve?—can be answered with the theory of identity proposed by Paul D'Ambrosio and me in *You and Your Profile: Identity After Authenticity*.[24] Here is a brief outline of this theory in relation to gender.

The conceptual core of *You and Your Profile* consists in the distinction between three "identity technologies"—that is, social and psychological practices by which we build our sense of self and ascribe selfhood to others: "sincerity," "authenticity," and "profilicity."[25] These three words are put inside quotation marks because the first and the second are used as technical terms and therefore convey a sense somewhat different from their common meaning. The third has been specifically coined to designate a rather new identity technology for which no proper existing term could be found.

Following Lionel Trilling, sincerity as an identity technology means finding selfhood in *sincere commitment*—behaviorally, emotionally, intellectually, etc.—*to social roles* including, importantly, gender roles.[26] As mentioned, in traditional societies many women internalized and enacted female roles (such as daughter, wife, or mother) in line with social expectations. They identified with such roles and were identified with them by others. This is to say, gender relations were organized along the lines of distinct, and typically hierarchical, gender roles.

Once more following Trilling, authenticity, as an identity technology, arose out of the revolt against a strict commitment to social roles. In modernity, such commitment increasingly appeared not as a good but as a bad thing: as mere *conformity*. In the "age of authenticity" (as Charles Tayler called it), personal identity was supposed to be found in the *pursuit of originality*.[27] "Originality" has several overlapping but also partly contradictory levels of meaning: being unique and special, being creative and innovative, and being unaltered, pure, or original in the sense of "from the beginning." Accordingly, individualism arose, and relations among humans were increasingly considered as oriented toward the mutual recognition of sovereign and autonomous agents, independent of their respective gender.

As argued in *You and Your Profile*, the age of authenticity is currently coming to an end, however, and a third identity technology is taking hold: the building of selfhood through the *curation of profiles*, or "profilicity."[28] In the case of successful profile curation, we become truly invested in our profilic identity. On social media and in our professional or political lives we tend to "brand" ourselves in certain ways and then hope that our profiles are validated through social feedback loops. Such social validation feedback loops often now characterize our relations with our "general peer"—anonymous larger audiences to whom we present ourselves, and with whom we interact, without meeting them in person.

Identity technologies are formative for making gender what it concretely is at any given time in history for any concrete person. When "sincerity" dominates, people identify with conventional gender roles. In the age of authenticity, rebelling against such gender roles is regarded as indicative of a person's unique individuality. In an almost dialectical way, profilicity combines the contradictions between sincerity and authenticity. On the one hand, the authentic idea of "being true to oneself" is celebrated and, on the other hand, identification with a collective gender identity once again takes on a positive meaning. Profiles tend to affirm gender and to emphasize its display. While the public display of gender identity under conditions of profilicity is somewhat reminiscent of the age of sincerity—for instance, by emphasizing gender in how people dress, speak, and move—profilicity differs from sincerity by dissociating gender from fixed roles. In profilicity, being a woman is no longer tied to being a wife or mother. Profiles can be freely mixed and matched, changed and reinterpreted. Profilic identity, including profilic gender identity, is dynamic, unpredictable, and diverse.

CHAPTER SUMMARIES

Working toward better narratives around gender is the purpose of this book. This work is undertaken with two philosophical resources that present alternatives to the premise of an essential individual self: Daoism and the theory of identity technologies. In connection with this theoretical endeavor, Daoism also promotes something practical: gender ease.

The first chapter provides an account of a Daoist philosophy of gender and identity. At the core of this philosophy is a critique of the early Chinese sociopolitical regime of sincerity associated with Confucianism. While Daoism shares with Confucianism a thoroughly relational conception of selfhood, it combats the internalization of (hierarchical) roles and regards human identity, including gender identity, as provisional and subject to transformation. The Daoist view on gender is embedded in the much larger and more comprehensive conceptual horizon of yinyang thinking. From a yinyang perspective, an essentialist, individualist pursuit of gender identity is absurd and potentially pathological. Accordingly, the Daoist approach to gender roles is not to *be* them, but to *play* them as enjoyably as possible.

The second chapter attempts to provide a philosophical theory of the self and gender identity. Although the self is scientifically elusive—it's impossible to pin down and define through empirical means—a sense of self is instrumental for individuals and society, enabling them to function. It is a crucial psychological, social, and existential construct, and it includes a personal sense of gender. The Daoist question here is how to be comfortable with one's gendered self despite all its incongruities and the contingencies of life.

The third chapter focuses on gender in non-Western contexts before and after the age of authenticity. One problematic aspect of current Western transgender narratives is that they tend to project the historically specific paradigm of authentic identity onto non-Western gender identities, such as "third genders" in Asia and elsewhere. Largely outside the scope of authenticity, however, non-Western gender identity has, at least in part, moved rather seamlessly from gender roles to gender profiles. Looking beyond the contemporary West can provide insights into how gender identities differ considerably when different identity technologies are applied.

The fourth chapter zooms in on current narratives and depictions of transgender in media, politics, medicine, and, especially, in law—because, arguably, transgender is at this point in history at the forefront of redefining gender as profile. An outline is provided, with reference to the transgender philosopher Natalie Wynn and her popular YouTube channel *ContraPoints*, for how transgender identity today can be lived and experienced in a profilic way. However, while transgender today arguably presents the most advanced form of gender profilicity, it is—as shown by Miquel Missé—also most burdened by the "identitarian" heritage of the age of authenticity. With reference to the theory of different identity technologies, the chapter attempts to clarify some misunderstandings and problematic assumptions around transgender today.

The conclusion wraps up the book with a short summary of its main points—and an outlook on how to be more at ease with gender in times of profilicity.

1

A DAOIST VIEW ON
GENDER AND IDENTITY

EARLY CHINESE "IDENTITY POLITICS"

Daoism is often understood today as a mystical philosophy that promotes harmony with nature and "going with the flow," or as a practice that cultivates bodily well-being, spiritual mindfulness, and tranquility with the aim of helping people to "be in touch with [their] real selves."[1] Such popular conceptions of Daoism are justified in one way or another, but they tend to be overly general and, moreover, to see Daoism through the lens of the age of authenticity—the modern (Western) concern with the "true self" and the pursuit of originality. This is to say, such "self-help" approaches tend to be quite detached from the historical context in which Daoist philosophy first emerged: pre-imperial China between the sixth and third centuries BCE.

There is a general agreement among scholars of Daoism that the first foundational Daoist text, the *Laozi*, was understood (although not exclusively) in pre-imperial China and during the Western Han dynasty (202 BCE–9 CE) as a political text. Like most early Chinese philosophical texts, the *Laozi* or, as it was later called when elevated to canonical status, the *Daodejing*—"Classical scripture of *Dao* [way, course, path] and *De* [virtue, power, vitality]"—functioned, as a sort of advisory manual for rulers.[2]

The second foundational text of Daoism, the *Zhuangzi*, also dates back to early China. Its earliest parts are traditionally attributed to the historically obscure philosopher Zhuang Zhou, believed to have lived in the fourth century BCE. Unlike the *Laozi*, parts of the *Zhuangzi* emphatically encourage its readers to avoid participation in politics. One of the most famous tales about Zhuang Zhou has him sarcastically refusing an offer to take on a highly paid government job. He compares state officials to sacrificial oxen that first get pampered and honored only to be eventually killed.[3] The story illustrates a core message that appears in various forms in many of the book's stories: being a politician is dangerous and tends to corrupt people or, worse, leads to their premature death.

At first sight, the *Laozi* and the *Zhuangzi* seem to represent two diametrically opposed takes on politics. While the former presents a vision of how to govern effectively, the latter critiques political involvement as potentially "dirty." The strikingly different attitudes to politics in the *Laozi* and the *Zhuangzi* can be understood as rooted, however, in a shared Daoist opposition to a mainstream consensus in early Chinese society. Both texts reject the assumption that social and political order and legitimacy rest on the congruity of "names" (*ming* 名) with "forms" (*xing* 形) or "actualities" (*shi* 实).

The political imperative of the coherence of names and forms can appear rather odd from a contemporary perspective where notions such as "democracy" and "human rights" appear as fundamental principles and practices of statehood. And yet the focus on names was of great importance in early China.[4] The Confucian *Analects* report that, when asked what his first priority would be if entrusted with the government, the Master (Confucius) responds, "Necessarily, the straightening of names!"[5] When asked by another questioner about the principles of government, Confucius sheds light on what is meant by straightening names: "Rulers must be ruler-like; ministers must be minister-like; fathers must be father-like; sons must be son-like."[6] If there had been "presidents" in early China, I might have translated the beginning of Confucius's pronouncement as "presidents must be "presidential," instead of the somewhat awkward locution "ruler-like." His point was that, just as order and functionality in the family depend fundamentally on members living up to their roles, order and functionality in the state depend on the same principle: each person must act, think, and feel in accordance with their position in society. Confucius was aghast to see how *un*ruler-like rulers of his time behaved. This is not so different from the feeling shared by some people today, that the unpresidential behavior of presidents ruins the global sociopolitical order.

The idea that names and forms need to cohere was also of categorical importance in early Chinese Legalism, the philosophical tradition that, along with Confucianism, has been at the heart of Chinese political thought and practice ever since. An emblematic story in the key Legalist text the *Hanfeizi* (third century BCE) illustrates this dramatically:

> Once in the past Marquis Zhao of Han got drunk and fell asleep. The keeper of the royal hat, seeing that the marquis was cold, laid a robe over him. When the marquis awoke, he was pleased and asked his attendants, "Who covered me with a robe?" "The keeper of the hat," they replied. The marquis thereupon punished both the keeper of the royal hat and the keeper of the royal robe.

He punished the keeper of the robe for failing to do his duty, and the keeper of the hat for overstepping his office. It was not that he did not dislike the cold, but he considered the trespass of one official upon the duties of another to be a greater danger than cold.[7]

Although set in different contexts, Confucius's proclamations in the *Analects* and the story of Marquis Zhao in the *Hanfeizi* express the same basic idea. That people thoroughly identify with their respective social roles, professional duties, and political titles—in how they act, think, and feel—is instrumental for establishing and preserving sociopolitical order. Roles, duties, and titles are the "names" (*ming*) that the forms, or per*form*ances, need to match.

The doctrine of correspondence between names and forms amounts to an early Chinese "identity politics" within the framework of what I call "sincerity." Names provide a normative and an existential orientation. Transplanted into an early Chinese context, Nietzsche's famous dictum "Become who you are!" (a variation on a saying by the fifth-century BCE Greek poet Pindar) would take on this meaning: Sincerely commit to the social roles and relationships, professions, and offices that you have been born into, that have been assigned to you, or that you have taken on. Names (roles) *are* identities.[8]

On multiple levels, early Daoist philosophy challenges the then mainstream idea—shared in principle by Confucians, Legalists, and other schools of thought—that a person must con*form* to their names. The Daoist critique of the doctrine of correspondence between names and forms is a critique of an early Chinese "regime of sincerity."[9] In my view, this critique is central to early Daoism and provides the grounding for its philosophy of ease and genuine pretending.

THE DAO HAS NO NAME

The book of *Laozi* consists of eighty-one enigmatic philosophical "poems" that are often difficult to make sense of and resemble divinatory texts, proverbs, or riddles. Its first two verses juxtapose the notions of *dao* 道 (the way, course of nature, or path) and *ming* (name). They can be translated as: "A *dao* that can be spoken of is not a constant *dao*. A name that can be named is not a constant name." Various readings of these lines have been suggested,[10] but whatever specific interpretation is preferred, it is clear that "names" are a major issue in early Daoism. The character *ming* occurs multiple times in nine of the eighty-one chapters. Most are variations on the theme of the namelessness and ineffability of the *dao*; and both chapters 32 and 41 explicitly state that the *dao* "has no name" (*wu ming* 无名). The text also implies, and *Zhuangzi* 1:3 explicitly states, that the "sage" (*sheng ren* 圣人)—the prototype of the ideal ruler—has no name either.

Given the great importance ascribed to names in early Chinese philosophy, the proclamations that the *dao* and the sage are nameless were quite provocative. To state that neither the *dao* nor the sage (the ideal ruler) has a constant (*chang* 常) name is to say they have neither a definite identity nor a specific role. Accordingly, Daoist texts, such as chapter 41 of the *Laozi*, often indicate that neither the *dao* nor the sage has a (constant or definite) form (*wu xing* 无形).

In the *Laozi* and other Daoist texts, the namelessness and formlessness of the *dao* and the sage are illustrated by a number of other negative qualities such as emptiness, stillness, and inactivity. All these negative qualities, however, are regarded as giving rise to their positive counterparts. Namelessness and formlessness beget names and forms, stillness begets movement, and inactivity begets activity. This idea is succinctly summarized in the final line of chapter 40 of the *Laozi*, "Presence is generated from non-presence," or, translated in the ontological terminology of Western philosophical traditions, "Being is generated from nonbeing" (*you sheng yu wu* 有生於无). Cosmologically, this model of generation is one of *emergence* rather than creation. Rather than stemming from a first cause or first mover, as in Aristotelian thought, whatever *is* originates in what *is not*. Unlike in Platonic or monotheist metaphysics, Daoism does not presume any ultimate idea, teleological purpose, or intelligent design at work behind what is. Behind everything that *is* is that which *is not*.

The cosmological and metaphysical primacy of non-presence over presence results in a paradoxical approach to politics: rulers are supposed to rule by not-ruling.[11] The most famous maxim of Daoist political theory is *wu wei* 无为, which translates as "nonaction" or "purposeless action." It occurs frequently in the *Laozi*. In accordance with this maxim, chapter 63 of the *Laozi* advises (the ruler): "Do the non-doing. Fulfill the task of no-task. Taste the tasteless." Accordingly, the aim of a ruler's Daoist self-cultivation is to empty their sense of self. In its equally enigmatic and poetic language, chapter 37 of the *Laozi* encourages prospective kings to overcome all their purposefulness by envisioning themselves as the "nameless uncarved wood" (*wu ming zhi pu* 无名之朴). Sage rulers have no name; their role is a paradoxical no-role and their identity is a paradoxical nonidentity.

The approach to political theory in the *Laozi* is rather mystical; it becomes much more concrete, and radical, in the *Zhuangzi*. While the *Laozi* advises the ruler to enact their political role in a paradoxical way as a non-role, the *Zhuangzi* advises its readers never to take on the role of a ruler, if at all possible, or any other government position for that matter. The pursuit of rank and titles is harmful. Chapter 5 of the *Zhuangzi*, for example, introduces a number of "freakish" characters who are at odds with social conventions. One of them is Toeless of Unk Mountain, an ex-criminal "whose feet had been mutilated as a punishment." He accuses Confucius of "seeking some bizarre, deceptive, illusory, freakish thing like a name and not realizing that the Utmost Person views such things as handcuffs and leg chains."[12] In another irreverent fictional narrative, in chapter 20, a person named Grand Duke Let-Be (Ren 任) meets a downtrodden Confucius in distress and admonishes him: "Who can get rid of fame and name? . . . Utmost Persons have no reputation. Why do you, Sir, so delight in such things?"[13]

Names, in the early Chinese sense of official roles and positions, are for the *Zhuangzi* "handcuffs and leg chains," which despised ex-cons are glad to have left behind, but toward which supposedly exemplary persons like Confucius still strive. In the same vein, the Daoist Duke Let-Be, who does not identify with his position of power, ridicules Confucius for his obsession with making a name for himself and "being someone."

The *Zhuangzi* rejects identification with names. It critiques the desire for rank and reputation as a pathological vanity—an obsession with ultimately meaningless designations. All names are provisional, the *Zhuangzi* suggests. The idea of a general incongruity between names and their referents is expressed in the formulaic statements "Names stop at actualities" (*ming zhi yu shi* 名止於实) and "Names are the guests of actualities" (*ming zhe shi zhi bin ye* 名者实之宾也).[14] Both proclamations seem to imply that names go only so far when it comes to determining someone or something. In the words of chapter 2 of the *Laozi*, names are not "constant." Neither exhaustive nor final, they are preliminary and inconsistent—and so is a person's identity.

The incongruity of names and forms or actualities is the theme of a crucial story in the so-called Inner Chapters (the first seven chapters of the *Zhuangzi*, which, some scholars claim, were written by Zhuang Zhou himself). The story has Yan Hui, a prominent disciple of Confucius, question his master about a person named Mengsun Cai, who in Confucius's home state Lu (representing here a Confucian society) is known as an exemplary mourner.[15] Mourning one's parents and ancestors was regarded as a prime manifestation of the core Confucian value of *xiao* 孝: affection and devotion to one's parents, traditionally translated as "filial piety." The practice of *xiao* demonstrated a person's commitment to their most central social role: that of a child to their parents. The proper emotional depth and behavioral accuracy in mourning one's deceased parents was the litmus test for sincerity. It showed whether a person was truly in line with Confucius's primary ethical and political demand that a son be son-like, and the mourning requirements for being truly son-like were somewhat extreme. To be considered properly *xiao*, one should observe a mourning period of three years after a parent's death and retreat from public life during this time.[16]

Contrary to the Confucian expectation of correspondence between names and forms, Mengsun Cai mourns without being overcome by sadness. And yet he is deemed a master mourner. Accordingly, a perplexed Yan Hui asks Confucius how it is possible that "someone who does not have the actuality still gets the name" (*wu qi shi er de qi ming* 无其实而得其名者). With the incongruous irony typical of the *Zhuangzi*, Confucius responds not as a Confucian but as a Daoist. He explains that Mengsun Cai understands the transience of everything. Consequently, he is able to show equanimity in the face of death, much like many other characters in the *Zhuangzi*, and to accept human mortality as the natural course of all things.

Embedded in a Daoist metaphysics of impermanence and change, the story of Mengsun Cai illustrates the difference between a Confucian and a Daoist philosophy of identity. From a Confucian perspective, the role-identity as child of one's parents is of categorical importance; it is regarded as *inviolable.*[17] In the worst-case scenario, that is, in the case of an Antigone-like conflict between family-based *xiao* and other moral duties concerning society at large, *xiao* must take precedence. A locus classicus illustrating this principle is a story about the legendary sage ruler Shun in the book of *Mengzi* (or *Mencius*, fourth century BCE). When asked in section 7A:35 what Shun would have done if his father, known as an evildoer, committed a murder, Master Meng replies that Shun would have accepted the apprehension of his father by the authorities in line with the law—but would have then "secretly carried the old man on his back and fled to the edge of the Sea and lived there happily, never giving a thought to the Empire."[18]

From a Daoist perspective, however, all role-identities are temporary and incongruent. Yes, on the one hand every person is a child to their parents and thus inescapably and intimately tied to them, both emotionally and socially. On the other hand, though, this relation is coincidental, temporary, and in constant flux; it is not everything a person has been, is, and will be. In fact, a person *is* nothing in particular but contingently "thrown" into (by birth) and out of (by death) relations. This includes the relation to one's parents. From a Daoist perspective, it is important not only to be able to enter and sustain such relations but also to be able to exit them.

On the one hand, Mengsun Cai indeed performed the mourning rituals and cried as he was expected to do. He was capable of emotionally and behaviorally fitting his role to perfection. And yet, when the role came to its end, his "heart-mind" (*xin* 心)

remained uninjured, as the text says—or, as a Buddhist would say, it was free from "attachment." The *Laozi*, on the other hand, presents an early Daoist philosophy of "nonattachment" that is primarily political and applied to rulers. Rulers will be most effective, and most cherished by their subjects, it is stipulated, the less they are personally attached to their ruler-identity. The *Zhuangzi* extends this approach to all social roles and to everyday existence. All roles, or "names," are temporary and do not define a person once and for all.

The story of Mengsun Cai illustrates the paradoxical idea that the skill of being able to "let go" of one's roles enables a person to enact these roles well (which Paul D'Ambrosio and I call "genuine pretending"). To practice nonattachment to one's roles was not easy when a powerful regime of sincerity, manifested in the categorical imperative of the correspondence between names and forms, dominated ethics and political thought in early China. But even today, in Western societies of the twenty-first century, it is still often difficult to let go of one's roles, especially in the case of parents and children. In early China, the notion of *xiao* emphasized the moral duty of the younger toward the older generation. Somewhat conversely, in contemporary Western societies, the duty of parent toward child tends to be emphasized. In some cases, the parent internalizes, and identifies with, their parenting role to a pathological extent. While writing this chapter, I read a CNN report of an Australian couple who nearly starved their teenage daughter to death in an attempt to prevent her from growing into an adult.[19] The parents acted, the report mentions, out of "love" for their child, and apparently wanted her never to cease being "little." While the story of Mengsun Cai in the *Zhuangzi* cautioned against an overidentification with "filial piety" in early China, the reporting of this tragic case implies a caution against an overidentification with parenthood.

FORGETTING ONESELF

Mengsun Cai, the paradoxical Daoist model son, exemplifies a paradoxical Daoist art of mourning a loved one's death without being overly sad. This is to say, he exemplifies a Daoist art of not overidentifying with one's identity. When describing Mengsun Cai's attitude toward life, the *Zhuangzi* uses the metaphorical expression *dan zhai* 旦宅, which Brook Ziporyn translates as "morning wakings to ever new homes."[20] This expression provides a clue for understanding Mengsun Cai's seemingly extraordinary mental, spiritual, and existential state. This clue is a very ordinary, mundane, and common experience—waking up in the morning.

Particularly when waking up from an intense dream, we might feel completely lost for a moment. On the one hand, we have already exited from the dream, we realize it was "only" a dream, and our memory of it recedes quickly. We cannot hold onto it; we must let it go. But on the other hand, we've not yet quite reentered our waking reality. We might not know where we are or, even more uncannily, who exactly we are. We may need to make a mental effort to be sure again of our home, age, marital status, job, or even our name. In this transitional "no-self" state where we don't really know who we are, we are from a Daoist perspective most truly (*zhen* 真) ourselves, in a nonauthentic, empty form.

During dreams, we are subject to the capricious workings of the unconscious (note, however, that this Freudian notion has no equivalent in Daoist philosophy), and after waking up we resume the personal identities that result from the random events in our lives. In our dreams and in our waking lives we must identify with these personas, even though they change all the time: not only do our dream-selves change every night, our daytime selves also change, albeit less drastically. We change from one day to another depending on what happens to us socially (we might fall in love, a war may start, our manuscript submission may get rejected), in our body (we grow and age, we may get sick), and in our mind (we happen to read a book on Daoism and see the world differently the next day). Only in the brief transitional moments between our dreaming and waking existences are we undetermined by the contingencies we encounter—we do not identify with them. These moments are, in a paradoxical way, the only moments in which we are "free" to be "ourselves"—by being free from any particular self. They provide short breaks from the inescapable identification with ever-changing selves that we inhabit in our dreaming and waking lives.

From a Daoist perspective, it is in such moments without identity between our dreaming and waking lives that we are "awake" (*jue* 觉). Mengsun Cai managed to extend this paradoxical state of nonattachment and was, according to the *Zhuangzi*, "especially awake" (*te jue* 特觉).

Confucius and Yan Hui's dialogue about Mengsun Cai is followed by another conversation between the two a little further down in the same chapter. Yan Hui seems to have practiced Mengsun Cai's art of de-association and cultivated it even further. He declares proudly that he is "making progress" and just "sits and forgets" (*zuo wang* 坐忘).[21] "It's a dropping away of my limbs and torso," he says, describing his experience of Daoist meditation, "a chasing off of my sensory acuity, dispersing my physical form and ousting my understanding until I am the same as Transforming Openness."[22]

Similar experiences are mentioned throughout the *Zhuangzi*. One of the most famous passages is the opening story of the second chapter, where a meditating Daoist master claims, "I have lost me" (*wu sang wo* 吾丧我).[23] Such physiological and spiritual practices have been one of the pillars of so-called Daoist religion (*dao jiao* 道教) for at least two millennia. However, the *Laozi* and the *Zhuangzi* highlight at least as much the philosophical, sociopolitical, and existential dimensions of the Daoist art of forgetting oneself.

Chapter 21 of the *Zhuangzi* includes the story of Sunshu Ao, who was three times promoted to high office only to be fired each time. He reacted each time with perfect equanimity, showing neither pride nor disappointment. When questioned about how he managed to maintain such calmness throughout these ups and downs, he explains:

> I just see whatever comes as impossible to refuse and whatever goes as impossible to retain. I merely looked on those gains and losses as having nothing to do with me. . . . I ask, does what matters reside in these external things or in myself? If in those things, it has nothing to do with me. If in myself, it has nothing to do with those things. So now all I do is dawdle at my ease, gazing about me in all directions—what leisure do I have to worry about whether people honor or despise me?[24]

The stories of Sunshu Ao and Mengsun Cai resonate with one another. Both protagonists not only demonstrate a Stoic calmness when facing hardships that are beyond their control; what is more, they distance themselves from their role identities and the social expectations tied to them. The "external things" Sunshu Ao refers to are the "names"—the roles, offices, and titles—he could neither refuse nor retain. Like Mengsun Cai, he managed to avoid clinging to these names or allowing them to define him in any way. Thereby, Sunshu Ao could say of himself, "All I do is dawdle at my ease."

THE TRANSFORMATION OF THINGS

The larger framework of the Daoist philosophy of the non-self in the midst of all our personas is a "metaphysics" of the "transformation of things" (*wu hua* 物化).[25] Probably *the* most famous Daoist allegory—both in China and abroad—illustrates this very concept: the Butterfly Dream story in the *Zhuangzi*. Zhuang Zhou fell asleep, the story goes, and was a butterfly in his dream, happily flying around. Once awake, there was Zhuang Zhou again, perfectly content. The text then quips that we can't know whether Zhuang Zhou became a butterfly in his dream, or a butterfly turned into Zhuang Zhou in his. There's certainly a distinction—literally, a "cut" (*fen* 分)—between the two, the allegory concludes, and "this is what is called the transformation of things."[26]

It is evident from the context and from interpretations of the story by traditional Chinese commentators that the depicted transitions from waking to dreaming stand for the transitions from life to death.[27] As is explicitly stated at the end, the story is meant to demonstrate that all things (*wu* 物), evidently including humans, change (*hua* 化). Any identity is temporary and the wherefrom and the whereto of all transformations are unknowable. Everything is subject to dissolving and reassembling in another form. Nothing is substantial.

As I have argued in other publications, the story has been seriously mistranslated and misinterpreted in the context of the rising age of authenticity since it was made available to Western readers.[28] In the "classical" translation by Herbert A. Giles, first published in 1889, the story is wrongly presented as if written from the first-person perspective, and the words "I," "my," or "myself" occur thirteen times.[29] In the Chinese original, the text consists of only 62 characters, and none of them is "I," "my," or "myself." The heavy emphasis on the "self," not just in Giles's translation but also in others, including James Legge's and in particular the influential German translation by the philosopher Martin Buber, suggests that the story depicts an ancient Chinese version of the modern Western struggle to find one's "real self" in a world where it is difficult to clearly distinguish between truth and illusion.[30]

Contrary to this reading, affirming the transformation of things does not imply a search for the authentic "I" that is "who we truly are" but hidden under various "masks" of ever-changing false appearances. Instead, it means more or less the exact opposite: there is no subsistent or authentic self at all. Selfhood is a temporary state, contingent on circumstances. There is no independent agency to be discovered "underneath" or "in between" states of self. There are just "morning wakings to ever new homes." In these moments of waking, as in the moments between an intense dream and being fully awake again, there is no identity.

Importantly, the affirmation of the transformation of things does not imply existential doubt, gloom, or forlornness in a world full of illusions. To the contrary, each transformation is equally real and valid in its own right. The Butterfly Dream story suggests that, from a neutral vantage point (and with a bit of humorous imagination), we may say with equal justification that a butterfly turns into a Zhuang Zhou in its dream and that a Zhuang Zhou turns into a butterfly in his. Both of them have the same *genuineness*. It is clearly true: When dreaming, we really exist. We have an altered consciousness then, for sure, often drastically different from our waking life. But we are just as bodily alive and mentally active as when awake. A psychoanalyst may even say that our dreams reveal more about ourselves than do the beliefs we consciously hold. But the Butterfly Dream story is not about the unconscious; it is an allegory suggesting that the alteration of selfhood that every person undergoes when asleep resembles, on a smaller scale, the radical alteration of selfhood in the transition from life to death. This transition does *not* mean a shift from reality to illusion or from being to nothingness, but instead the shift from one reality—or better, from one identity—to a different one.

Another story in the *Zhuangzi* has a group of Daoist friends joke about how their bodily matter will transform after their death: one arm may become a rooster, the other a crossbow, and so on.[31] In a lighthearted manner, both the Butterfly Dream story and the story of the Daoist friends say: There is nothing to fear or worry about the dissolution and reconfiguration of selves and bodies; this is the natural course of things (or of the *dao*), and each identity, although distinct or "cut" off from those before and after, can be happy and content in its peculiar fashion.

The main "protagonist" of the Butterfly Dream story, the butterfly, symbolizes both radical transformation—it transforms from a crawling caterpillar into a flying creature—and unperturbed happiness, manifest in its joyful fluttering. Zhuang Zhou, too, is depicted as happy and untroubled. Importantly, the text explicitly states that the butterfly does not know of Zhuang Zhou, and the same is clearly implied vice versa. Precisely *because* each is unaware of the other, neither questions their "true self" and both are carefree. Their happiness is tied to the Daoist art of forgetting oneself.[32]

EASE AND PLAY

The shift in focus from the central theme of life and death to a concern with "me and myself" is not the only issue with Western authenticity-oriented mistranslations of the Butterfly Dream story. An arguably even greater distortion is that readers are presented, and left with, the impression of Zhuang Zhou as a Daoist philosopher who is heavily absorbed in introspection and, presumably, scratching his head in deep existential puzzlement. This impression obscures, or even reverses, the *mood* of the original story. The key "plot" of the original story, shown in countless Chinese paintings over the centuries,[33] involves one or more butterflies flying about almost weightlessly while a completely relaxed man dressed in loose garments takes a casual nap under a tree or in some other natural setting. It's a mood of perfect lightness, of thoughtlessness, and of *ease*.

The Butterfly Dream story not only allegorically illustrates the transformation of things; more importantly, it provides relief from the fear of death, and conveys—like the Chinese paintings depicting it—a feeling of playfulness, contentment, and comfort while forgetting oneself.

Promoting a state of ease is a common thread in Daoism and especially in the *Zhuangzi*. The theme of ease permeates Daoist political philosophy, and the philosophy of the namelessness of the *dao* and the sage, through commending *wu wei*, or "purposeless action." It permeates the sociopolitical and existential critique of the regime of sincerity by commending dissociation from roles and ranks. And it permeates the Daoist philosophy of identity—the "metaphysics" of the transformation of all things through life and death—by commending, in various forms, the art of forgetting oneself. The *Zhuangzi* describes ease in numerous ways, but one expression is used about one hundred times throughout the book and occurs in the title of the first chapter, *Xiaoyao you* 逍遥游. This title has been translated variously as "enjoyment in untroubled ease" (James Legge), "going rambling without destination" (A. C. Graham), "free and easy wandering" (Burton Watson), "wandering far and unfettered" (Brook Ziporyn), and "carefree wandering" (Victor Mair). The key Chinese character rendered as "enjoyment," "wandering," or "rambling" is *you* 游. It means moving around leisurely. In contemporary Chinese, it is contained in the words for "swimming" (*you-yong* 游泳) and "tourism" (*lü-you* 旅游). In the figurative sense found in the *Zhuangzi*, as in the expression *xiaoyao you*, its main connotation is that of being playfully at ease.

The existential state of playful ease is beautifully depicted in another famous story in the *Zhuangzi* featuring Zhuang Zhou as a protagonist. Here, Zhuang Zhou and his best friend, Huizi, who also happens to be a philosopher, are strolling along the river Hao.[34] Seeing some fish swimming in the river and apparently enjoying themselves, Zhuang Zhou says, "This is the happiness of fish!" This prompts Huizi to state that Zhuang Zhou, since he is not a fish, cannot know that the fish are happy. A short dialogue ensues. Zhuang Zhou turns Huizi's argument against him: since Huizi is not Zhuang Zhou, he is in no position to claim that Zhuang Zhou cannot know that the fish are happy. The friendly banter goes on a little further without a clear resolution of the question. Neither of the two friends conclusively wins the argument.

Most contemporary scholarly interpretations of the story zoom in on the contents of the dialogue between Zhuang Zhou and Huizi and ascribe different epistemological positions to them. These interpretations typically ignore what I believe is the central theme of the story: existential ease and playfulness. In the original Chinese text, the character used for Zhuang Zhou's and Huizi's "strolling" as well as for the "swimming" of the fish is *you*. As mentioned, this character has a strong philosophical significance in the *Zhuangzi* and signals right away the *mood* of the story. The carefree happiness of the fish in the water mirrors the animated intellectual conversation between the two friends on land. Both—the fish and the philosophers—*go nowhere in particular*. This is to say, neither the zigzagging of the fish nor the back-and-forth of the philosophical dialogue arrive at a definite aim or conclusion. Both are "going rambling without destination" (as A. C. Graham translates *xiaoyao you*). And this is the point of the story: rather than defending one epistemological view against another, it illustrates that fish can be at ease by swimming around playfully just as philosophers (or humans in general) can be at ease by playfully strolling around and debating. As in the case of the Butterfly Dream allegory, pictorial depictions of the happy-fish story in Chinese paintings typically capture quite well—unlike most scholarly interpretations—this mood of playful ease.[35]

Comparing paintings of the Butterfly Dream allegory and of the dialogue on the happiness of fish reveals a key similarity between the two stories: both place the playfulness of animals in parallel with human ease. The fluttering butterfly mirrors the snoozing Zhuang Zhou, and the swimming fish mirror the strolling and bantering friends. Via their mood and imagery, both stories vividly depict the core of the Daoist philosophy of identity. It is not a quest to "become who you really are" or "be in touch with your real self." It is rather about "being at ease with whoever you happen to be." A main idea of this book is to show that this Daoist approach to identity can also be applied to gender. But before addressing this topic, I wish to say something more about humans, animals, and genuine pretending in Daoism.

HUMANS, ANIMALS, AND GENUINE PRETENDING

The resonance between humans and animals depicted in both the Butterfly Dream allegory and in the story of the happiness of fish can easily be related to current environmental philosophy and animal ethics. In a paper included in the volume *Daoism and*

Ecology, E. N. Anderson argues that the story of the happiness of fish is meant to show that "people and fish share enough basic similarity that humans can understand them."[36] Accordingly, Anderson writes, the story's message is that "in a deep and basic sense, Dao unites humans and animals, and teaches us to treat them with respect.[37] Such readings make sense today, but they are somewhat anachronistic. They run the risk of invoking the spirit of the age of authenticity by, to an extent, humanizing and individualizing animals. To say that humans can "understand" fish and therefore need to "respect" them because of a "basic similarity" is to apply the larger conceptual framework of modern human rights to animals. In this reading, the happy fish appear almost as rational and autonomous agents who, according to ethical principles, must be recognized as somehow humanoid. The relation between humans and animals is framed as a kind of intersubjectivity, reflecting a contemporary tendency to regard animals as "companions" or "pets" and to treat them as family members. If I understand the *Zhuangzi* correctly, however, such an attitude to animals was far from the minds of its authors and of its readers in early China. The resonance between fish, butterflies, and humans that the stories in question doubtlessly implicate is, in my reading, of a different kind: it is based on a mutual letting be and a noninterference with species that are distinctly nonhuman. And yet, the butterflies and fish in the *Zhuangzi* do mirror humans, but in a *metaphorical* sense. The resonance between Zhuang Zhou and the fish or the butterfly does not indicate a human–pet relation; it is, I believe, a symbolical expression of the Daoist philosophy of genuine pretending. When realizing genuine pretending, we can experience the playful ease that we see in fluttering butterflies or happy fish.

To appreciate the philosophical and metaphorical meaning of animals in the *Zhuangzi*, it is essential to situate the text in its

historical context and to understand how it employs animal allegories as a sociopolitical critique of early Confucianism.

In its own metanarrative, the Confucian tradition portrayed
itself as overseeing a grand civilizational process that gradually
transformed a wild and disorderly world into a cultured order.
Paradigmatic outlines of this narrative are included in the book
of *Mengzi*. According to the *Mengzi*, the world was initially
"flooded" (*fan lan* 氾濫) with water (in a manner somewhat
similar to the biblical scenario).[38] The first great civilizational
act by pre-Confucian sage rulers was the regulation of rivers
and the separation of the human habitat from the inundated
earth. The second obstacle that needed to be dealt with was the
flora, the "grasses and trees" (*cao mu* 草木) growing everywhere.
These were kept in check by carving out from the wilderness
an agricultural space to be cultivated by humans. Still, "birds
and beasts [*qin shou* 禽兽] encroached upon men."[39] Another
sage king eventually took care of this predicament; he "set the
mountains and valleys alight and burnt them, and the birds
and beasts went into hiding."[40] Hence the wild animals were
expelled from the human realm. However, the purification of
the human world from the flora and fauna was still not
sufficient—the "inner animal" had to be purged as well. The
Mengzi says that once humans "have a full belly and warm
clothes on their back they degenerate to the level of animals if
they are allowed to live idle lives, without education and discipline."[41] To combat this inner beastliness the first "minister of
education" imposed the five "human relationships": (*ren lun* 人伦)
between fathers and sons, between rulers and ruled, between
husbands and wives, between older and younger siblings, and
between friends in society. Only by imposing this structure of
role-relationships was the separation between humans and animals complete.[42]

The grand Confucian civilizational process consists of an ever more thorough cleansing of the human realm from everything that is wild and disorderly. This process goes from the expulsion of "grasses and trees" and "birds and beasts" to a human self-disciplining by means of largely hierarchical power structures tying people to their relational roles (manifest in the "names" *father* and *son*, *husband* and *wife*, etc.).

Another central early Confucian text, the *Xunzi* (third century BCE), echoes the *Mengzi* in claiming that the supposedly unique capacity to establish a social order through role distinctions is what distinguishes humans from wild animals: "What make humans human? They have divisions. . . . . Birds and beasts also have fathers and sons, but they do not have the familial bond between them. They have males and females, but they do not have the distinction between man and woman."[43] According to another passage in the *Xunzi*, it is precisely the hierarchical order of humans that enables them to cooperate with one another and to domesticate the animals not driven out from the human realm: "Humans are not as strong as bulls and not as fast as horses, but they make use of bulls and horses. Why? Because humans can associate and they cannot."[44]

From an early Confucian perspective, the animal kingdom can be divided into two categories: undomesticated wild animals that pose a threat to human civilization and domesticated animals that are dominated by and for humans. (To my knowledge, pets do not occur.) The presentation of animals in the *Zhuangzi* reacts to precisely this pattern—in a deeply critical and subversive way.

Chapter 29 of the *Zhuangzi* presents a bitterly ironic counter-version of the Confucian master narrative of the grand civilizational process and the domestication of animals. This critique is put into the mouth of the early Chinese archvillain Gangster

Zhi, the infamous leader of a large group of outlaws. In a diatribe scolding Confucius, Gangster Zhi says that in the times prior to the Confucian sage rulers, "People slept where they happened to be and woke up cheerfully. They knew their mothers, but they didn't know their fathers. They lived side by side with the deer. . . . This was when the utmost vitality was in abundance." But when the Confucian sage rulers appeared, they "slaughtered the native tribes out in the wild, and their blood ran for a hundred miles. . . . Since then, the strong have always oppressed the weak and . . . brought disorder to humankind."[45]

It has been suggested that Ganster Zhi is a spokesperson for a Daoist "primitivism."[46] But it seems clear to me that his character is far too ambiguous and exaggerated to be taken as a straightforward Daoist. To me, the function of the grotesque figure of Gangster Zhi in the *Zhuangzi* is not to argue in earnest for a return to a pre-civilizational state of nature where people lived a nomadic life, had casual sex and no families, and cohabited with wild animals. Instead, his persona is a literary device for a drastic deconstruction of the Confucian-civilization story. Its grandiose self-description, Gangster Zhi suggests, is a bogus pseudohistory and far from the truth. The imposition of the Confucian social order by no means made people happy. In reality, the Confucian regime was a violent, corrupt, and suppressive system making almost everyone suffer a more or less permanent state of unease.[47]

Symbolic critiques, in the form of animal allegories, of the rigid and repressive Confucian regime of sincerity are found throughout the *Zhuangzi*. There is a whole narrative genre in the text that can be classified as "kill stories," which tell of the sometimes brutal, sometimes bizarre, and sometimes unintentional killing of animals and other nonhuman creatures through acts of domestication or "civilization."[48]

One such kill story is about Bo Le, a legendary horse expert who is commonly portrayed in other Chinese texts as an exceptionally skilled master. In the *Zhuangzi*, however, he is a villain. He boasts that he is good at "ordering" (*zhi* 治) horses, a choice of words that connects him with the larger political project of the Confucian tradition.[49] Contrary to Bo Le's claim, the *Zhuangzi* depicts him not as improving the lives of his horses but, by subjecting them to strict training exercises, killing almost half of them. Somewhat similar to Gangster Zhi's diatribe, the *Zhuangzi* explicitly likens Bo Le's murderous treatment of horses to the, often equally deadly, treatment of native populations by the Confucian-civilization regime that disciplines humans with "ritual and music" (*li yue* 礼乐) and "humaneness and righteousness" (*ren yi* 仁义).[50] (There is an eerie parallel between how the *Zhuangzi* depicts the extermination of tribal people through the Confucian-civilization project and the genocides of indigenous populations in the context of "Christianization.")

Horses and cows (and bulls and oxen, which in Chinese are all called *niu* 牛) are a *pars pro toto* representation of domesticated animals in early Chinese texts (e.g., in the *Xunzi* passage about horses and bulls quoted above). As mentioned, a well-known legend has Zhuang Zhou rejecting an offer to take on a government post because he does not want to end up like an ox killed at a royal ritual. The symbolism is clear: just as domestication injures or kills horses and bovines, the sociopolitical framework of Confucian role hierarchies kills humans. Domesticated horses and cows are metaphors for the social identities Daoists try to avoid. Daoists identify instead with wild animals escaping domestication such as fish, birds, and butterflies. But wild animals are also under threat and can be hunted and killed. One allegory even has Zhuang Zhou himself hunting a bird (only to eventually be hunted in turn as a poacher).[51] Another story tells of an exotic bird caught and later inadvertently killed while being hosted as a guest of honor at a ruler's court.[52]

While not immune to danger, fish, birds, and flying insects benefit in the *Zhuangzi* from their "uselessness"—they can survive because they remain outside the "civilized" space characterized by functions, roles, and names. The very first chapter of the book—which, as mentioned, is titled *Xiaoyao You* (Carefree wandering)—begins with a fantastic depiction of the mythical fish Kun and the mythical bird Peng. Kun is of an enormous size and transforms into the equally gigantic Peng. Like the Butterfly Dream allegory, this is an obvious symbol for the core Daoist idea of the "transformation of things." What is more, the Kun-turning-into-Peng animal also symbolically represents the state of *you*: "Spiraling aloft with the whirling winds, he ascends ninety thousand miles into the sky, availing himself of the gusty breath of the midyear to make his departure."[53] Exceeding by far all human proportions, Kun-Peng is utterly beyond domestication and manifests "wandering" in a most monumental dimension.

The *Xiaoyao You* chapter is of great poetic richness and philosophical complexity. It presents a host of elusive allegorical creatures and characters. These figures represent, in various stages of perfection, the "wandering" (*you*) that is "nowhere brought to a halt" of the "Utmost Person" who "has no definite identity" (*wu ji* 无己), the "Spirit-like Person" who "has no particular merit" (*wu gong* 无功), and "the Sage" who "has no name" (*wu ming* 无名).[54] The conflict between *you* and the concern with "identity," "merit," and "name" is a central theme in the *Xiaoyao You* chapter. It is exemplified in the description of the philosopher Song Rongzi (also known as Song Xing). The *Zhuangzi* says that Song would "burst out laughing" at anyone "whose understanding is sufficient to fill some one post, or whose deeds meet the needs of some one village, or whose personal virtues please some one ruler." This is because, for Song, "if the whole world happened to praise [him], he would not be goaded onward; if the whole world condemned him, he would not be deterred."[55] Song Rongzi does not buy into the Confucian regime of sincerity. According to the *Zhuangzi*, neither do the native tribes of the remote region Yue. The text tells of "a ceremonial cap salesman of Song traveling to Yue, where the people shave their heads and tattoo their bodies—they have no use for such things."[56] The ceremonial cap salesman stands for the attempt to "civilize" people into a regime of sincerity, while the shaved heads and tattooed bodies of the people of Yue symbolize the "wild" state of *you*.

As in the case of the grotesque Gangster Zhi, "uncivilized" people and undomesticated creatures often described in fanciful poetic hyperbole are key symbols of *you* in the *Zhuangzi*. This symbolism must be understood as a literary device. Commending *you* does not necessarily mean that readers of the *Zhuangzi* are encouraged to emigrate to Yue, shave their heads, and tattoo their bodies or to dive deep into the ocean and then rise high into the sky like Kun-Peng. In the early Chinese regime of sincerity and its "identity politics" of names and forms, commending *you* has the much simpler implication of encouraging people to *play* their roles without attachment to them—this is genuine pretending.

Most appropriately, Lisa Hamm, the cover designer of *Genuine Pretending: On the Philosophy of the Zhuangzi*, chose an image of a fish to illustrate the theme of the book.[57] In Daoism, fish, birds, and butterflies symbolize, on the one hand, genuineness. Unlike domesticated animals, such as horses and cows, fish manage to avoid instrumentalization for a function imposed on them. A Hegelian might say: they avoid "alienation" by humans, a species that is *other* to them. Fish remain *truly* fish by *not* being identifiable with a role in the human fabric. Moreover, being fish, and thus presumably thoughtless, they don't even identify "as fish." Their genuineness corresponds to the genuineness of the "Utmost Persons" whom the *Xiaoyao You* chapter says "have no definite identity." This genuineness allows them, unlike workhorses, to move around playfully and, seemingly, happily. Humans, too, can experience such states of "useless" and joyful movement, especially in their childhood when playing. The word "pretending" can refer to such play with toys or puppets. When children play, they are "genuinely pretending." When adults play their roles, they are genuinely pretending as well, but they tend not to admit it.

Early Daoism came to understand that, in a way, everyone, including the world of adults, is genuinely pretending. Everyone plays a role but "has no definite identity." Under a regime of sincerity, however, where everyone is pressured to identify with their name-roles in the social hierarchy, people tend to live in denial of this fact. People *pretend to be genuine* instead—they become victims of the "ceremonial cap salesmen," so to speak, and believe that they really *are* the role that the cap they have been sold indicates. Once this is the case—once we seriously identify with the caps we wear rather than, like children, merely play with these identities for a while—the capacity to be at ease like a fish is severely diminished.

DAOISM AND "GENDER IDENTITY"

I put "gender identity" in quotation marks in the title of this section because there was hardly any concept of gender identity, in the contemporary sense, in early Daoism or indeed anywhere in early China. The concept of gender identity commonly shared today is by and large individualistic: we tend to assume people *are*, in themselves, female, male, transgender, etc. Gender identity is often regarded as an inherent aspect of a person's "own" identity. In early China, however, as was arguably the case in any society characterized by a regime of sincerity, identity and gender identity tended to be conceived relationally. The relational conception of gender identity is visible in a traditional but still commonly used word for "women" in Chinese, *funü* 妇女. It literally means (as in *Zhuangzi* 14:6 and 29:1) "wives and daughters."

The American Confucian philosopher Henry Rosemont Jr. has described the individualistic concept of personhood metaphorically as a "peach" and the relational one, which he regards as Confucian, as an "onion."[58] The peach represents the idea that a person has a pit at its center—the core-self. Everything else around the core-self, a person's body, history, and social attributes, are like the fruit and the skin of a peach, layered around the pit and enclosing it. The pit is the singular seed of it all; it is the *true* self. The onion, on the other hand, has no pit; it consists of multiple layers without a center. "What is left when there are no more layers?" Rosemont asks. "Nothing at all."[59] The layers of the Confucian "onion-self," according to Rosemont, are human role-relationships: a person is a child of one's parents, a spouse of one's spouse, a friend of one's friends, etc. The self grows by growing more and more relationships throughout one's life. Importantly, the self cannot be abstracted from these relationships: a person never is, and has never been, an isolated, singular self.

Reflecting a relational rather than an individualistic understanding of gender identity, early Chinese texts rarely identify people simply as "a male" (*nan ren* 男人) or "a female" (*nü ren* 女人). Instead, men are often introduced with reference to where they come from (e.g., "a person from Lu"), or by their title (e.g., "the Grand Duke of Wei"). Women are often introduced as "the wife of" or "the daughter of" someone. This indicates that the gender identity of a person was not commonly understood in a "peach" way, as an isolatable aspect of a person's individual "pit," but rather in an "onion" way, as embedded in multiple layers of social roles and relationships.

As indicated above, the common view on gender relations in early China was strongly patriarchal—particularly, but by no means exclusively, in the Confucian tradition. A passage reflecting the patriarchal ideology of the time also made its way into one of the not so Daoist-sounding chapters of the *Zhuangzi* (a text that elsewhere tends to be iconoclastic):

> The ruler precedes, the subjects follow. The father precedes, the sons follow. The elder brother precedes, the younger brothers follow. The elder precedes, the younger follows. The male precedes, the female follows. The husband precedes, the wife follows. The hierarchies of honored and lowly, first and following, are the activities of heaven and earth, and thus the sage takes their image as a model.[60]

The early Chinese locus classicus expressing the role-related subordination of women to men is a passage in the ritual text *Dadai Liji* (compiled during the second century CE) that defines the "three obediences" (*san cong* 三从) women ought to practice: as daughters, they need to obey their fathers; as wives, their husbands; and as widows, their sons.[61] This implies, conversely, that the role of men is to always exert authority over their female family members. Typically, texts on gender identity in traditional China outlined in a moralistic fashion the mutual obligations and behavioral norms of men and women within such a hierarchical pattern. An early example focusing on the submission of

women to men is the *Lessons for Women* (*Nü jie* 女诫), written by
Ban Zhao, a woman who lived in the first century CE. Texts
such as these served as educational materials and were often
memorized.

Given the primacy of the relational conception of human
identity in ancient China, the early Daoist approach to gender
also focuses on relations rather than on individual identity in the
modern sense. This approach is often critical. One example of a
critique of patriarchal gender relations in the *Zhuangzi* is Gangster Zhi's abovementioned diatribe against the Confucian
civilization-process. When the gangster claims that in the good
old days before the Confucian regime of sincerity, people "knew
their mothers, but they didn't know their fathers," he clearly indicates that the "three obediences" did not yet apply: women grew
up without fathers, they had no husbands, and therefore they
never became widows. Even if, as I believe, Gangster Zhi was a
literary persona and his diatribe should not be mistaken as an
argument for abolishing families, the text still subverted the
mainstream conception of gender identity that existed at the time
and invited readers of all genders not to internalize the harsh
hierarchical gender roles imposed on them by early Chinese
society.

Chapter 14 of the *Zhuangzi* includes a dialogue between Laozi
and Zigong, one of Confucius's most famous disciples. Quite
similar to Gangster Zhi's dressing-down of Confucius, Laozi
berates Confucius's representative Zigong for his naïve belief in
the Confucian civilizational saga. Like Gangster Zhi, Laozi
completely revises the standard narrative and gives an opposing
account of how the power grab by Confucians gradually destroyed
human well-being. In the beginning, Laozi says, at a time when
the (still Daoist) Yellow Emperor ruled, "when someone didn't
cry at the death of his parents, nobody blamed him." Before

Confucianism, Laozi implies, people could easily be like Meng-sun Cai, not needing to be *xiao* or to overidentify with the role of son or daughter. This changed with the first Confucian sage ruler Yao. He introduced *xiao*—and then bloody vendettas spread: "When someone killed the killer of his parents, no one blamed him." The situation got worse when Shun, the next Confucian sage ruler, took over. Everyone became highly competitive and overambitious, and people "began to die young." During the time of the sage ruler Yu, things got so bad that warfare was common and "the world was gripped in great terror." At this stage, Laozi says, "there first came to be the whole idea of ethical roles and relationships, the result being that now men have to take daughters as their wives."[62] As Brook Ziporyn explains, Laozi can be understood here as saying that "marrying a woman now requires recognizing her as the daughter of her father and thus entering into the network of familial relationships" or that "it could be a reference to incest."[63] In any case, Laozi makes the point that the establishment of role-relations was the culmination of a long history of increasing human suffering. He particularly emphasizes how the gender-role identities of daughter and wife corrupt men and injure women. Hierarchical role-identities, and in particular the unequal gender roles in the family, make life miserable for everyone.

It is probably worth adding that the *Zhuangzi* makes fun of a key aspect of the feminine role: women are expected to embody "female beauty" to attract men. In the context of an allegory ridiculing (and relativizing) human value judgments, an odd Daoist sage humorously named King Kid (Wang Ni 王倪) brings up two of the most famous "beautiful girls" of early China: "Humans regard Mao Qiang and Lady Li as great beauties—but when fish see them they dart into the depths, when birds see them they soar into the skies, when deer see them they bolt away without

looking back. Which of these four 'knows' what is rightly alluring?"[64] The story humorously illustrates that beauty standards
are social constructs and thereby suggests they should not be
taken all too seriously. Moreover, by once again contrasting
"civilized" humans with wild animals, it may also imply that
beauty standards are not needed for procreation, and that it may
well be possible to enjoy sex in a "wild" way without them.[65]

YINYANG

It is impossible to talk about gender in Daoism without addressing yin and yang—an early Chinese conceptual pair that has
become one of the most famous "memes" associated not just with
Daoism but, rightly so, with Chinese philosophy as a whole.
While related to what we today call "gender," the expression has
a much more complex range of meaning, far exceeding the
notions of female–male and feminine–masculine.

In her brilliant monograph on the subject, Robin R. Wang
transcribes the expression *yin-yang* 阴阳 in one word as "yinyang," reflecting "the Chinese usage in which the terms are
directly set together and would not be linked by a conjunction."[66]
As Wang outlines, yinyang is a "paradigm" consisting of two
components that should not be regarded as individual parts
but as a *relation*.[67] This paradigm sets up "a horizon for much
of Chinese thought and culture," which also encompasses the
conceptions of identity and gender in early Daoism outlined in
the preceding pages.[68] Within this horizon, *everything* is seen
relationally and subject to transformation, including gender
identity.

The yinyang framework can be traced to the earliest canonical
texts in Chinese history, the *Book of Documents* (*Shang Shu* 尚书)
and the *Book of Odes* (*Shi Jing* 诗经), which date back (at least in

part) to the first half of the first millennium BCE. In these texts, the terms "yin" and "yang" refer respectively to the shady (northern) and sunny (southern) sides of a hill.[69] In the following centuries, the yinyang terminology spread throughout early Chinese cultural production and permeated most philosophical discourses. As Stephan Feuchtwang writes, yinyang has been "seen in all forms of change and difference such as the annual cycle (winter and summer), the landscape (north-facing shade and south-facing brightness), sexual coupling (female and male), the formation of both men and women as characters, and sociopolitical history (disorder and order)."[70] This list is by no means complete.

In addition to being relational and processual, yinyang is contextual, or *contingent*, and so, Robin R. Wang says, "a single thing can be yin in one way and yang in another." She then explains, beginning with a quote from the sinologist Alfred Forke:

> "The left hand is Yang, the right hand is Yin, in this no change is possible, but raise both hands, then they are both Yang, and put them down, and they are both Yin, and no matter whether you raise them or put them down, when they are hot, they are both Yang. And when they are cold they are both Yin." . . . It would be absurd to argue whether the right hand is *really* yang or *really* yin. The qualities only make sense when one specifies a certain context. The fact that anything is simultaneously yin and yang mirrors the fact that things are always implicated in multiple relations at once. Moreover, which relation is in view depends on the particular purposes and priorities of the viewer.[71]

Rather than conceiving of yinyang as dual "principles," as is often stated, it may be better to understand it as a notion of two *moments* constituting a relational and processual context. The *contingent* relations between the two moments, as Wang illustrates in great detail, can take at least six basic forms: (1) contradiction and opposition (*maodun* 矛盾), (2) interdependence (*xiangyi* 相依), (3) mutual inclusion (*huhan* 互含), 4) interaction or resonance (*jiaogan* 交感), (5) complementarity or mutual support (*hubu* 互补), and (6) change and transformation (*zhuanhua* 转化).[72]

The complex yinyang framework of the six relational types listed by Wang was also applied to the dynamics of social roles, including gender roles: husband (yang) and wife (yin) can have opposite hierarchical positions—which are especially emphasized in the Confucian tradition—but are also mutually dependent and complementary to one another. They interact with and, to an extent, include each other (for instance, as parents, when a mother also has fatherly aspects, and vice versa). Moreover, gender roles change and transform with aging, which is understood as a process from yang to yin.

Although the yinyang dynamic was applied to social relations, it remained non-anthropocentric. Yinyang is not a specifically human notion; rather, as stated in chapter 42 of the *Laozi*, "all things (*wan wu* 万物) carry yin, embrace yang." In this vein, when the *Laozi* emphasizes female powers by stating that "the female (*pin* 牝) overcomes the male by constant stillness" and advises the sage ruler to "maintain the feminine (*ci* 雌),"[73] the respective terminology (*pin* and *ci*) does not indicate "women" but the wider category of "female" in the context of all animals. As in this case, when Daoist texts thematize the male–female distinction, they often do so in the context of the larger, naturalistic yinyang horizon rather than in the specifically human gender-role context emphasized in the Confucian texts.

On the one hand, the yinyang horizon—which has a strong presence in Daoist texts—and the hierarchical gender-role framework characterizing early Confucianism share a common relational approach. Neither yinyang nor the man–woman relation in early China pertain to the inherent "gender identity" of individuals in a modern sense. Instead, both view what we now call "gender" as a contextual relation. To paraphrase Robin R. Wang, from a yinyang perspective it would be absurd to argue about whether a single individual was *really* yang or *really* yin. And, from the perspective of a Confucian role hierarchy, being "male" or "female" says little about a person; instead, their "gender identity" consists concretely in the various *roles* they are expected to perform in relation to one another.

On the other hand, however, the yinyang framework provided an important philosophical background for the critique of the rigidly patriarchal gender politics in early China promoted in Confucian and other texts. These rigid politics were enacted through a regime of sincerity expressed in the imperative that names must correspond with forms. "Names" established a normative pattern of (gender) roles associated with particular (gender) per*form*ances. The yinyang framework enabled Daoist writers like the authors of the *Zhuangzi* to realize that those roles did not need to be reified and internalized as personal identities but that they could be taken to be and enacted as contingent and subject to transformation. This is to say, Daoists understood that the roles with which we identify, including our gender roles, are genuinely pretended—and so, at least potentially, can be played with ease. The question is: can we develop a similarly critical understanding of, and, arguably even more importantly, a similarly playful attitude toward, our gender *profiles* today?

2

A SHORT THEORY OF THE SELF
AND ITS GENDER

FROM THE IMMORTAL SOUL TO THE
SOVEREIGN INDIVIDUAL—AND BEYOND

The introduction to this book documented how the enigma of the gendered self haunts current narratives about gender identity. It seems few people have a clear idea what this concept actually means, despite its huge (and often divisive) media presence and political impact. The critical analyses by Masha Gessen and Miquel Missé help to achieve some clarity about currently dominant views on gender identity. They illuminate three assumptions that underly how gender identity is commonly conceived: it is inherently individual, it is essential (i.e., something a person really *is* by themselves), and it is something a person should (be empowered to) get right.

The first chapter, on gender identity in Chinese philosophy, showed that gender narratives are by no means universal, however. For instance, gender identity can be viewed relationally in terms of gender roles, rather than individualistically. These gender roles can be considered as binding, as in Confucianism, or as contingent and transitory, as in Daoism.

Such major differences between divergent narratives about gender are best explained, I argue, in relation to different identity technologies. The ages of sincerity, of authenticity, and of profilicity condition how we build a gendered sense of self—our gender identity. Before sketching a theory of the self and its gender, I intend to trace the relation between identity technologies and notions of identity and gender in Western philosophy and religion. On the one hand, unlike in China, powerful discourses in premodern Western philosophy and religion centered on an explicit notion of *individual* selfhood in terms of an immortal soul.[1] On the other hand, as in China, these discourses were embedded in a regime of sincerity that conceived of (gender) identity as *asymmetric* and hierarchical or, more precisely, as shaped by patriarchal role-relationships.

"Individual" literally means that which is indivisible and cannot perish. It stems from the Latin word *in-dividuus*, which in turn corresponds to the ancient Greek word *a-temnein*, or "un-cuttable," from which the word "atom" is derived. An understanding of individuality, in the sense of immateriality and thus indestructibility, was attached to the early Greek notion of the psyche, or "soul," which strongly influenced the conception of selfhood in Christianity—and beyond.

Plato's *Republic* ends with Socrates recounting at length the "myth of Er."[2] Er was a soldier who died in battle. When his soul was released from his body and went to the underworld, the judges there made him return to the living so that he might reveal to them the secrets of life and death. According to Er, the underworld consists of two different realms, one for the souls who did good in their previous lives, and another for those who did evil. After some time, most souls are released again and must come back to earth. First, though, they take part in a complicated procedure for selecting their next body. The procedure involves a combination of chance and choice and is supervised by several goddesses. Socrates explains with respect to the element of choice that the most philosophical souls, and therefore the wisest, make the best choices while the meanest souls make the worst. Once their new bodies have been assigned to them, the souls must leave the underworld by crossing the Plane of Oblivion, where they need to swim through the River of Lethe. *Lethe* means "forgetfulness," and by drinking from its water all souls completely forget their experiences of the underworld and their past lives. The souls are then reincarnated in their assigned bodies in a state of amnesia. They must acquire all knowledge and wisdom once more from scratch.

The myth of Er has numerous levels of philosophical and religious meanings and allows for complex interpretation of the nature of the soul. It encapsulates in narrative form the larger framework of a mind–body dualism that characterizes both Platonism and (some understandings of) Christianity: the soul is immortal, whereas the body must die. The soul is immaterial and spiritual—it has rationality and emotionality—and causes the material body to be alive. It is the life principle of the body. Because of its spiritual qualities, the soul is able to guide the body; through learning and practice it acquires moral qualities and intellectual powers. However, weak souls will not be able to control the body and instead are controlled by it. Evil and unwise souls may lead the body astray. In the afterworld, the weak and evil souls are punished. Moreover, they are likely to make bad choices for their next lives, and so their ill consequences are perpetuated on earth.

Central philosophical and religious motifs in the myth of Er are still preserved in contemporary notions of the self. Even if the self is no longer conceived of as a soul, it is still commonly thought of as an immaterial (and potentially immortal) agent that inhabits the body as its mental and emotional owner. The self is supposed to have the capacity to steer the body and to make morally good or bad decisions. Accordingly, it also bears responsibility for the person's actions and is deserving of reward or punishment.

In ancient Greek philosophy, as in Christian religion, the soul-self is not completely free, however. It can make choices, as in the myth of Er, but it is also subject to chance. Ultimately the soul-self is in the hands of goddesses and gods—or, in Christianity, of the one supreme Almighty—and dependent on them for mercy. The soul-self has a certain degree of responsibility for what it does with its body, which makes it eligible for judgment by the gods or God. But at the same time its agency is limited and, at least to an extent, determined by divine powers. It is fated, or "meant," to do what it does. It is guided by an intelligence higher than its own, whose influence and supervision it cannot escape and whose rationale is difficult if not impossible to fathom. The premodern individual has immortality, but it lacks sovereignty.

Plato's individual soul-self not only lacks sovereignty, it also lacks both sex and gender. In the Myth of Er, souls can be reincarnated in bodies that are radically different from the bodies they had in previous lives. A soul that animated a female body can animate a male body the next time around, and a soul that inhabited an animal can inhabit a human being in the future, or vice versa. The immateriality of the soul made it immune to sexual differences and, by extension, to gender differences; as in the ancient world, long before Simone de Beauvoir, the notions of sex and gender were not yet differentiated.

In Christianity, souls are not reincarnated in different bodies; there is no transmigration of the soul, no metempsychosis. A common belief in Christianity is that once immortal souls are separated from the body through death they go eventually to heaven or hell, where they are bound to stay. Since the Christian soul is just as immaterial as Plato's, it must also be sexless, it would seem. In a recent theological monograph titled *On Gender and the Soul: An Exploration of Sex/Gender and Its Relation to the Soul According to the Church Fathers*, Eastern Orthodox scholar Benjamin Cabe confirms this assumption, saying that "the sexless soul is and remains the *consensus patrum*."[3] According to Cabe, the church fathers agreed that the soul had neither sex nor gender. A traditional source that makes this very point is the *Catechetical Lectures* by Cyril of Jerusalem (fourth century CE). In the fourth of the lectures, Cyril said, "The soul is immortal, and all souls are alike, both of men and women; for only the members of the body are distinguished."[4]

And yet, the sex of the soul is by no means an uncontroversial topic in Christianity. When it comes to the resurrection of the souls, numerous religious renaissance paintings, such as Michelangelo's *The Last Judgment*, show those in heaven or hell, or those on their way, as males or females rather than as sexless. Apparently, the resurrected soul has a sex and is gendered. Moreover, modern Christian theologians challenge the traditional belief that the soul is immortal and purely spiritual. In his book *Philosophical Theology and Christian Doctrine*, Brian Hebblethwaite points out that "the idea of the soul's immortality as disembodied state beyond death is not popular amongst Christian theologians or among Christian philosophers today."[5] If there is no disembodied soul, the self, as designed by God, may well be gendered after all. Despite all theological efforts, the ways of the Lord remain mysterious, and He still withholds a clear pronouncement on the question of whether the soul has a sex and is gendered.

Although the theological question of a gendered soul-self remains undecided, it is obvious that in the Judeo-Christian tradition the male–female distinction was regarded as divinely created. Genesis 2:21–2:24 makes this abundantly clear:

> So the Lord God caused a deep sleep to fall upon the man, and he slept; then he took one of his ribs and closed up its place with flesh. And the rib that the Lord God had taken from the man he made into a woman and brought her to the man. Then the man said, "This at last is bone of my bones and flesh of my flesh; this one shall be called Woman, for out of Man this one was taken." Therefore, a man leaves his father and his mother and clings to his wife, and they become one flesh.[6]

The divine distinction between man and woman is a sex and gender distinction at the same time, combining biological and social aspects. The biological aspect of the distinction is highlighted by woman's (Eve's) creation from man's (Adam's) rib (or "flesh and bone") and the implication of procreation ("becoming one flesh"), while the social aspect is emphasized by mentioning that woman becomes man's *wife*. Irrespective of the question of whether their souls or only their bodies have sex and gender, the binary sex and gender role distinctions between men and women are deeply anchored in the Judeo-Christian creation story.

The biblical creation story depicts a peculiarly asymmetric relation between man and woman that reflects traditional patriarchal hierarchies. Eve is created out of Adam's rib. Thereby, as social theorist Niklas Luhmann says, the male sex/gender gains precedence over the female because it "maintains continuity with the origin" and "guarantees the systematicity of the new structure."[7] In the terminology of Simone de Beauvoir, the female is the *second* sex, created out of the primary and "original" sex, the male. The male sex, Luhmann states, has the "function of the representation of the system within the system."[8] This is to say, God is the *father* (not the mother), and *He* (not She) created humankind as *man*kind. Within the system of mankind, He further created the distinction man–woman in which the man part represents the whole. For Luhmann, this asymmetry mirrors the hierarchies characterizing premodern societies. In societies that were organized around a center–periphery distinction, the center (manifest in a capital city or royal palace) represents the whole, as does the highest rank (emperor or king) in a stratified or feudal society. Against the background of such hierarchical relations, the assumption of a hierarchical sex/gender difference between two kinds of selves made sense. Male selfhood and female selfhood were part of the same whole and yet *not* the same. The asymmetrically gendered self fits the regime of sincerity very well. On its own, the idea of an individual and presumably sexless soul provides little grounding for a relational, hierarchical concept of identity. The addition of a male–female distinction was necessary, it seems, to establish a thoroughly gendered sense of a role-self enclosing the soul-self.

Along with the transition to modernity and the shift from a regime of sincerity to the age of authenticity, the soul-self was eventually released from its relational role encumbrances and, what is more, from divine steering, oversight, and discipline. But the secularization, liberation, and emancipation of the self came at a high price: It traded its afterlife for its freedom. In the old world, the individuality of the soul-self guaranteed its immortality. In the new world, the meaning of "individuality" changed and began to indicate the autonomy and sovereignty of the self.

A paradigmatic text representing this shift is Immanuel Kant's famous essay "An Answer to the Question 'What Is Enlightenment?' " It begins with a succinct (double) definition: "Enlightenment is man's emergence from his self-imposed immaturity.

Immaturity is the inability to use one's understanding without guidance from another."[9] In essence, Kant's point is that enlightenment consists in the transition from an immature, or childish, state of selfhood to a mature state of selfhood where the individual is no longer dependent on others—especially not intellectually. The enlightened individual, Kant continues, is able to use their "own understanding" and can think for themselves. Here, the meaning of individuality lies in having reason as one's defining quality and being able to use it by *oneself.* While the shift in meaning from individuality as indestructability to individuality as an independent intellectual agent may be traced further back—for instance, to Descartes and his famous definition of the self as a "thinking thing" (*res cogitans*)—Kant's definition of the enlightened individual is decidedly this-worldly. Intellectually, the individual is no longer dependent on divine guidance, mercy, or control. Individuals are perfectly able to generate their own laws—they can rely on their own innate mental powers to understand what is right and what is not. (And whether these powers are thanks to God doesn't really matter since, according to Kant, whether God exists is unknowable). In short, the modern self has moved from *heteronomy*, or being subject to the laws imposed on it by others, to *autonomy*, self-determination by means of reason: *sovereign* individuality. For Kant, modern society is, or ought to be, a self-organized community of intellectually mature, autonomous selves.

In tight conjunction with the philosophy of authenticity, Kant's conception of the autonomous individual contains a developmental aspect. While humans are born with reason, they need to learn how to make use of it correctly. The intelligent self exists a priori but it needs to grow up in the real world to become truly autonomous. Guidance by others is at first still necessary but, as reflected in the ideal of contemporary Western education, it should ultimately be aimed at enabling the guided selves to eventually guide themselves.

Having emerged out of the premodern literal soul-self, the modern metaphorical soul-self is still regarded as a primarily spiritual, conscious, intelligent entity: it thinks and feels and inhabits a body. While it has lost its imperishability, it is empowered with free will and has been ascribed inviolable dignity. If nourished properly and empowered to exert its autonomous agency, it will thrive. The more control it has over itself—in other words, the more it can be self-determining—the more perfect is its selfhood.

Kant, the Enlightenment, and the age of authenticity in its "classical" form preserve the old Platonic-Christian mind–body divide. Selfhood is grounded in the power of reason, and reason is immaterial. Being immaterial, it is also sexless. In the twentieth century, it also becomes increasingly genderless. Along with the shift from a relational to a sovereign and autonomous self, the ties to social roles, including gender roles, are gradually dissolved.

Kant's famous essay on the definition of enlightenment includes a notorious remark on gender that is simultaneously sexist and not. Kant wrote that "the entire fair sex" regards "taking the step to maturity as very dangerous."[10] On the one hand, this is to say that *all* women have remained in a childish state of not fully reasonable individuals—which is a clearly sexist statement. On the other hand, though, he faults religious and political authorities for the alleged backwardness of women. He clearly implies that the traditional power structures and role assignments were designed to prevent women (and humans in general) from reaching maturity and fully reasoning selfhood. In other words, Kant criticizes sexism. Furthermore, while he generally affirms the morality and legality of patriarchal structures in society—and in this way was sexist—he also defines reason as universally human and not sex- or gender-specific. When he declares *Sapere aude* (Dare to use your own understanding) to be the motto of the Enlightenment, this appeal addresses everyone irrespective of their gender.[11] For Kant, as well as later for Simone de Beauvoir, selfhood lies in being an autonomous, rational human individual rather than in a person's "gender identity." In Kantian terms, sovereign individuality has a "transcendental" root, while gender is empirical. This view on gender identity characterizes the age of authenticity: Gender roles do exist, but they do not get to the origin of a person's selfhood and they can prevent an individual from being truly themselves.

Luhmann describes the overcoming of the traditional asymmetric relational conception of gender identity from his systems-theoretical perspective. He writes that the old "stratified differentiation" in feudal societies was replaced, in the period from the sixteenth to the eighteenth century, by what he calls "functional differentiation." Although in modern society differences between strata or classes still persist, they are no longer the most basic defining social differences, he suggests. Instead, at its most basic level society is now separated into different "function systems," such as politics, law, economy, academia, and the media. These systems, Luhmann suggests, are not subordinated to one another but instead constitute social environments for one another. Politics happens within an economic, legal, and media environment. At the same time, the economy develops in the context of whatever is transpiring in politics, law, media, etc. No system is intrinsically of a higher order than the others. According to Luhmann, within those social systems, traditionally stratified and patriarchal hierarchies lose their "plausibility."[12] Politicians, bankers, lawyers, and academics need not be differentiated or hierarchically ordered in relation to gender or sex. Instead, new hierarchies arise based on systemic criteria: politicians win or lose elections, bankers make or lose money, lawyers win or lose cases, and all this happens largely independent of their gender. Given these systemic dynamics, Luhmann says, the old hierarchical gender semantics "must be replaced by a semantics of equality."[13] If, along with the replacement of traditional role-relations by social-function systems, sex/gender differences lose their importance in modernity, and if gender thereby doesn't make a decisive difference anymore with respect to social ranking, then it makes sense to assume that the self is not gendered. This is precisely what the age of authenticity stipulated: the original self is individual and not defined by the gender roles and relations of the past.

Today, however, we are moving into the age of profilicity, where gender differences can once more matter greatly. On the one hand, following the logic and the new semantics of "functional differentiation," genders are considered equal and the old gender roles are a thing of the past. And yet, on the other hand, it is evident that gender does make a difference in one's *profile* as a politician, as an academic, or on Tinder. Reflecting the importance of gender for profiling oneself in any given social system, the assumption of a gendered self gains popularity anew. It is not surprising that it is currently makings a comeback, for example, in the claim that transgender people have gendered souls that were incarnated in the wrong body. This new profilic idea of gendered self is still often attached, however, to the older Kantian Enlightenment idea that it must also be autonomous and capable of "self-determination."

Recently, a friend shared a philosophy meme. It shows cartoon images of numerous philosophers proclaiming what "everything is." Thales says, "Everything is water!" Descartes says, "Everything is Mind and Body!" Spinoza says, "Everything is God!" The final philosopher in the meme is Ludwig Wittgenstein. He is depicted shrugging his shoulders and saying, "Actually it turns out metaphysical speculation is stupid, and this has all been a huge waste of time!" One could imagine a similar meme about the self. Plato might say, "The self is the immaterial and indestructible soul!" Confucius might say, "The self is in one's relations with others!" Cyril of Jerusalem might say, "The self is made by God and has no sex!" Kant might say, "The self is the mature and autonomous individual!" A contemporary transgender person might say, "My gendered self is trapped in the wrong body!" This would continue until finally someone would say, "It turns out that metaphysical and theological speculations about the self are pointless, and especially those about a gendered or sexless self." Candidates for the cartoon thinker making the last statement would be Robert Sapolsky or Natalie Wynn.

THE INSTRUMENTAL SELF

In one of her YouTube videos, the transgender philosopher Natalie Wynn points out straightforwardly, "I wasn't born a woman; I was born a fucking baby."[14] We might similarly say: We are not born as selves, we are born as babies. When human beings are born, they have neither a "peach-self" nor an "onion-self." From an empirical perspective, there is neither a soul-self nor any other kind of self. The self has no substance: It can be traced neither materially nor ideally to any core "entity." It is not one "thing" that can be "reified."

And yet, all readers of these lines, as well as their author, do think of and talk of them*selves* in terms of a self. The idea of a self is deeply engrained in our thoughts and language. As

Descartes famously outlined in his *Meditations*, whatever we think about, we think of it as thought by "me." Kant later formulated a variation on the idea by conceptualizing the "ego" or the "I think" as the "transcendental unit of apperception." He wrote in the *Critique of Pure Reason*, "The 'I think' must be able to accompany all my mental representations [*Vorstellungen*]."[15] But on further reflection, we observe this not to be exactly the case. When we are born, we do *not* think, "I think I've just been born." While we say in hindsight "*I* was born on this or that day," the *I* was not in fact yet present on that day. What do we make of this contradiction between firmly conceiving of oneself as a self on the one hand and, on the other, the impossibility of pinning down what exactly that self is, where it comes from, and when it begins and when it ceases to exist?

Psychological assessments of when exactly a sense of self develops in young children vary. It tends to depend on how the sense of self is defined. A sense of self may be expressed emotionally (in feelings about oneself, such as shame), cognitively (in distinguishing oneself from others or in recognizing oneself in a mirror), or linguistically (in referring to oneself in language). One account, approaching the sense of self through a study of emotions, says: "Generalized feelings of self-consciousness (typically labeled as an early form of embarrassment) do not develop until around 18 to 24 months. . . . More complex self-conscious emotions, such as shame, guilt, and pride, emerge even later, possibly by the end of the child's third year of life."[16] There are many other methods for ascribing a sense of self to humans (or animals). Regardless, there is a general consensus that the self is not innate, not present at birth, and that it develops over a person's life.

Humans do not simply acquire *the* self at some point in their lives. Instead, they learn to think, feel, and talk in terms of being a self when they grow up. The same is the case for a person's gender identity. In an academic encyclopedia entry on gender identity, Gregory K. Lehne writes:

> Gender identity develops through a process of differentiation: interactions of biological, social, and cognitive-learning factors that occur over time. . . . The child begins to develop a body image of the self as a girl or a boy. After the child acquires language, by eighteen months to two years, the child can label the self as girl or boy. This is the early expression of gender identity. Learning of some aspects of gender identity occurs at biologically sensitive periods of time; once learned, it is difficult to alter.[17]

Along with the psychologically complex development of a sense of self, a sense of the gender of this self develops. And although the sense of self as such and its gender identity may be "difficult to alter," both do change considerably throughout a person's lifetime. While, on the one hand, I still see myself as the same person I was when I was a toddler, I also see myself, on the other hand, as quite different—especially if I realize that I didn't even have a sense of self when I was born. Furthermore, being male means something different to me now from what it did when I began to identify myself as a boy when I learned to speak.

The self is neither essentially given nor static. It is a *construct* that varies depending on how it is constructed, observed, or ascribed, and by whom or what. It may be associated with a person's mind, with their body (including their brain), or their social persona or "character"—or with a mix of all of that. The sense of self "in us" emerges through social and psychological feedback mechanisms and has a bodily dimension. We think of ourselves as our*selves* not because there is a true self (or a soul) within us that we discover or create (as was claimed in the age of authenticity), but because we are treated as having a self by those around us. For instance, we learn a language that makes us use a personal name and the pronoun "I." Just as it is difficult, or even impossible, owing to the lack of a precise definition of what the self is, to determine exactly when a sense of self appears in a human individual, it is difficult or impossible to assess when exactly humans as a species began to develop selfhood. Did the early *Homo sapiens* some 300,000 years ago have a sense of self? And if so, was it similar to our sense of self today? And if it was similar to our sense of self today, was it similar to the sense of self of a two-year old child today or of a grown-up?

The sense of self changes not only over long periods of time but also on a daily (or nightly) basis. When we fall asleep, we temporarily lose our sense of self. When we dream, it is altered, muddled, or weakened, but once we wake up, we tend to still think of ourselves as the same self that slept or dreamt. Just because something is constructed and unstable is of course not to say that it is unreal. The value of the money in my wallet is also constructed (in actuality it's just a few pieces of paper and metal) and it is unstable (currency value fluctuates), and yet these pieces of paper and metal can really buy me things.

Selfhood emerges ontogenetically and phylogenetically in an individual human and in the species, respectively. It cannot be traced back to any divine origin, or any specific material or immaterial essence. Like everything else about humans, it has biological, psychological, and social aspects that mutually influence one another. But there is no self that can be distilled from these components and their unceasing mutual dynamics. In his recent book *Determined*, neurobiologist Robert Sapolsky uses the term "religious mysticism" to describe pseudoscientific attempts to find a self that steers an individual, such as John Eccles's books *Evolution of the Brain: Creation of the Self* and *How the Self*

Controls Its Brain.[18] The notion of a distinct agent called "self" with its own characteristics and powers has no scientific basis whatsoever.

We, as individuals and as a society, form notions of the self, and conceive of ourselves and others as selves, but in fact whatever we think, say, or do is not traceable to any ultimate "subject." What we think, say, or do results from numerous heterogenous factors contributing to it. The self is not at the bottom of "who we are." To the contrary, it is a surface interpretation of ourselves. It is a linguistic, semantic, metaphysical, or religious shortcut that pretends to explain largely unknown biological, psychological, and social processes that constitute us and our behavior.

Sapolsky introduces *Determined* with an anecdote about a conversation between a professor and a simpleminded student confronting him with the hypothesis that the world "is on the back of a gigantic turtle." When the professor questions her where that turtle stands, she says "on the back of another turtle." And when further questioned where that turtle stands, she replies, "It's turtles all the way down."[19] The student's seeming stupidity, however, turns out to be rather smart. Unlike Descartes in his *Meditations*, today's science no longer searches for an "Archimedean point" on which everything else rests as its ultimate cause. Likewise, science also does not reduce human behavior to any self at its foundation. Instead, human behavior stems from ever-emerging interrelations between our body, our mind, our society, our history, and so on. It's a heap of living turtles, so to speak, with no bottom and no top. Effects of the ever-moving stacked "turtles" can be traced in numerous directions. Biology, psychology, and society all contribute to and influence one another in forming human behavior.

Sapolsky conjures up a concrete example to illustrate the complexity of human behavior, effectively covered up by the notion of the self as autonomous agent. A driver needs to make an instant decision on whether to let another car merge into his lane on the freeway. If he decides not to and instead speeds up, we typically ascribe this decision to him—to his self. Instead, Sapolsky says, the decision is the "outcome of influences from one second ago to millions of years ago," such as the following:

> You're hungry. There was just a mysterious throbbing pain on the left side of your butt, and you're briefly worried that you have left-side-of-your-butt cancer, and thus feel entitled to drive selfishly. You're going to an important meeting and can't be late. You've gone a few months without getting a decent night's sleep. In middle school way back the tough kids bullied you a lot, and from that you have a vague, unspoken belief that letting someone merge in front of you on the highway equates to your being an inadequate pushover. It's the time of day when your testosterone levels are elevated, thus strengthening the signaling of neurons in the "I'm a weakling if I let someone merge in front of me" circuit (regardless of your sex). You have this or that variant of this or that gene. You're male and a member of a species in which there's a moderate but significant correlation between male-male competition and male reproductive success.[20]

As empirical science shows, such factors ranging from evolutionary biology to gender-based bias to short-term neurological states "determine" (or, better, condition) a simple action like the pushing of a pedal. And yet, out of mental habit, social convention, and ignorance about science, we tend to ignore all that in everyday life and simply assume that "the driver" did it—we commonly think his self was in charge.

From a strictly empirical perspective, Sapolsky seems undeniably right that there is no such thing as a self in the sense of an agent equipped with free will who inhabits our body and is, via mental activity, behind everything we do and is therefore "who we are." But equally undeniably, the psychological and social *construct* of such a self not only exists, but also matters. This very construct, in turn, can be regarded as just another psychological and social factor that—in combination with the evolutionary biology, the brain physiology, the genetics, etc., discussed by Sapolsky—significantly influences individual behavior and social functioning.

Take the economy, for example. From a "radical Sapolskian" view, the functioning of the economy must be explained very differently than from a humanist conception. The latter will assume that all economic activity can be traced back to "sovereign individuals" and their decision-making. Sapolsky would counter that each person's economic actions are instead "determined" by their brains, genes, emotions, etc., over which they have no control. While the Sapolskian approach is probably correct, it is also important to note that the functioning of the modern capitalist economy is based on the notion of private property. The concept of private property in turn assumes that there are selves who, as economic subjects, possess goods, engage in trade, have debts, and so on. Today's economy couldn't function as it does without the concept of personal owners—a concept that presupposes that an owner has a self.

Individuals today see them*selves*, and cannot but do so, as owners, for example, of a bank account. Some of my psychological worries result from looking at my bank account. When looking at it, I may feel that I, my*self*, lack money. I am not a neurobiologist, but from what I know through Sapolsky, I understand that my psychological worries about *me* lacking money have some sort of effect on what goes on in my brain. This shows that the concept of the self is not *just* a vain metaphysical

shortcut by which humans incorrectly ascribe free will to themselves. It is also a social and psychological idea that has very real
effects, for example, on one's brain chemistry. The construct of
the self enables humans to do real stuff, such as making and
spending money, and be worried about it.

For better or worse the sense of self evolved in humans (and
perhaps to an extent in other animals) as a psychological form
or *instrument* that fundamentally shapes the way we think, feel,
and communicate—all human languages, to my knowledge,
have words for, or functional equivalents to, "I" or "self." Unsurprisingly, self-related thinking, feeling, and communication has
also significantly shaped social evolution. Social systems, such
as the economy, politics, law—you name it—all assume the
existence of selves. While some societies may assume "onion-
selves" and others "peach-selves," it is difficult, if not impossible, to imagine a society that lacks any assumption of selfhood.
And since society, psychology, and biology mutually influence
one another and coevolve, the notion of selfhood also influences the development of the mind and body (including the
brain).

Again, Sapolsky is right: There is no empirical self, and much
less a metaphysical or religious self who is an agent of free will
and center of the sovereign individual. There is no sovereign
individual to begin with. *All* human behavior, including all
decision-making and intellectual and creative production, is contingent on biological, psychological, and social circumstances.
But at the same time the psychological sense of self and the social
concept of selfhood (or personhood) are formative modes of
human functioning, both on the individual and the collective
level. On the one hand, the pushing of the pedal in a car cannot
be scientifically ascribed to any entity called "self"—but, as
humans, we probably couldn't drive or have traffic as we know

it (with its laws, regulations, etc.) if we didn't have a sense of self: it's *instrumental, not essential*. If we didn't think that our self (although it's a mere construct) could drive a car, then we probably could not have developed this particular skill. And yet, as this example also indicates, the sense of self, while instrumental *for us*, is also *contingent*. It is already foreseeable that in the future cars will mostly be self-driving—or, more appropriately put, cars will be *self-less* driving machines.

CONTINGENCY AND INCONGRUITY

The sense of self supplies humans with the useful illusion of being in control and having free will, at least to some extent. The traditional metaphysics of the soul-self—as in Platonism and Christianity—located it in the mind or the spirit, which were tasked with enacting self-control over the body. It was assumed that by mentally or spiritually guiding our bodies we could avoid "sin." Secular approaches, like the abovementioned book *How the Self Controls Its Brain* by John Eccles, present a nonreligious and amoral version of the same idea of self-control. Mind–body dualism typically implied the goal of leading the body with the mind—and the fear that if such leadership was not achieved, the mind might be misled, subjugated, or perverted by bodily desires and emotions. In the seventeenth century, René Descartes outlined such a position in great detail in his treatise *The Passions of the Soul*. "Passions" in this context referred to emotions that were supposedly imposed on the soul as long as it was in a *passive* state in relation to the body. The soul ought to overcome this passive state by making correct use of its mental or spiritual powers and thereby become an active agent reigning over the body. Today it is still commonly assumed that the mind is, or ought to be, able to exert "willpower" over the body to prevent it from doing evil or harm.[21]

The depiction of the mind–body relation as a zero-sum struggle for control is, from a contemporary scientific perspective, largely fiction. As Sapolsky maintains, our decision-making is triggered by innumerable factors, ranging from the neuronal activity in our brains immediately before we act to genetic factors that, with origins far back in time, are mostly unknown to us and beyond our cognitive influence. Human decision-making is "always already" embedded in bodily and social contexts that individuals have no control over—and never could have.

The conception of the mind as an agency of the self that ought ideally to guide the body gave rise to Kant's Enlightenment vison of shaping human society according to the correct use of reason. In reality, however, mental, bodily, and social processes are evolutionarily intertwined and *condition* rather than guide one another. Just as human psychology is conditioned by physiological and social triggers, the body and the brain react to what goes on in the mind and in society. Society in turn is influenced by what people think and by what goes on in their bodies and brains. Rather than striving for control over one another, these different autopoietic (i.e., according to Luhmann, self-reproducing) systems—bodies, minds, society—are contingent on one another. They depend on one another to evolve and function the way they do. What is more, they are also contingent in the sense that they don't completely determine one another: the future remains open and unpredictable. The feedback mechanisms between biology, psychology, and the social world are so complex that there is no "root cause" that could inevitably steer evolution toward a specific effect—it's a heap of moving turtles.

If we think of the relation between the mind, biology, and society in terms of mutual contingency rather than in terms of a struggle for control, we can also dismiss the resulting fear that a "weak" mind will be helplessly ruled by the body. Mutual contingency means that *no one* is in control. There is no creator God before, and no commander within, evolution. The absence of an essential self and the contingency of the mind on its body and society does not mean that the mind is completely subjected to external powers. When someone writes a book, they write it thinking of themselves as its author—thinking of themselves as having a self—and they imagine with some justification that they will have some impact, however small, on what other selves think and do and on how they live. This has been the case with Sapolsky. Although he radically rejects free will and a self from a scientific perspective, he nevertheless insists throughout *Determined* that society and humans can change for the better, and he explicitly intends his book to contribute to bringing about such change. Paradoxically, although the self does not essentially exist, it is, as a social and psychological illusion, also *instrumental* for evolutionary change. The construct of a self is shaped in various forms, such as the peach-self or onion-self, and by various technologies, such as sincerity, authenticity, and profilicity. It is shaped by society, by our minds, and by our bodies (brains), and it shapes them in return.

The sense of self is based not just on contingency—in the double sense of being *contingent on* the coevolution of life, society, and the mind, and of *having no definite essence* and appearing in varying forms—but also on incongruity. Psychologically, we are exposed to widely differing and often conflicting emotions. In Sapolsky's example of the driver deciding whether to let another car merge into his lane, the man is conditioned in these few short seconds by multiple conflicting thoughts and feelings before he eventually accelerates or brakes. The decision is not predictable but is influenced by a vast multitude of different, largely unrelated, and coincidental factors, ranging from evolutionary biology to how many hours the man slept the night before. It depends on random circumstances. Accordingly, there is no ultimate "fit," no correct match, between the decision and its maker, and no unified rationale shared by them.

The life of a person consists of a chain of contingent events and decisions that do not constitute a coherent picture. Although, in hindsight, and in line with the illusion of the "sovereign individual," we each construct a narrative of a consistent self, such a narrative can be easily deconstructed by someone else by means of its contradictions. We typically see one another differently from how we see ourselves. Everyone has a different perspective on everyone else. A whole profession has emerged to deal with the contradictions of our self-narratives: psychotherapy. Self-narratives are, by definition, subjective, and their storylines are very much contingent on their teller.

There is neither an internal coherence to a person—we have dissonant feelings and contradictory thoughts—nor an external coherence to a person's social experiences. We do not seamlessly fit into the family and society into which we are born, and we are exposed by chance to shifting political, economic, and historical situations. We find ourselves "thrown" into utterly contingent and "absurd" circumstances, as existential philosophers of the twentieth century such as Heidegger or Sartre outlined at length. We are not the authors of our fate. The same goes, of course, for our bodies. There is no fit between our skin color, our height, our weight, and our age. These chance characteristics do not make up a congruent whole, and, moreover, they change rather randomly over time. The constructed self exists in unstable social surroundings, its body constantly changes its features, it is exposed to contradictory emotional triggers, and its thoughts and beliefs are often inconsistent. Although it may seem a mission impossible to delineate a congruent self in the face of such randomness and diversity, we manage to do so. We feel that all those different aspects of ourselves, ranging from how we look, what happened to us during our lives, and what we think and feel somehow belong together and, in combination with one another, present a neat picture of who we are—like the pieces of a jigsaw puzzle that eventually all fall into place. The identity technologies of sincerity, authenticity, and profilicity are social and psychological tools by which we perform this miracle of transforming existential dissonance into seemingly coherent selfhood.

GENDER AND SEXUAL ORIENTATION

A major part of the jigsaw puzzle that constitutes the illusion of the congruent self is one's gender. Gender metaphysics and gender theology, which contain the assumption that there is something essentially male or female in a person beyond their biological sex, can lend credibility and solidity to one's self-perception. Such an assumption makes the self more tangible and convincing. That I *am* a woman or a man (or a third gender person) seems then to be an obvious and undeniable fact, especially under social conditions where a strong gender metaphysics or theology prevails. In a society with a powerful regime of sincerity and where strong role conformity is prescribed to women and men (and potentially to a third gender), individuals will likely form a strong sense of gender identity. Where women and men are expected by their peers to live up to gendered roles, many will internalize the expectations and identify with them. But developing a strongly gendered sense of self as, let's say, a woman and not a man doesn't mean that one *is*, essentially, completely, and coherently feminine and not masculine.

Arguing against an all too binary gender metaphysics and theology, YouTube philosopher Natalie Wynn sees "masculinity and femininity as a duality inherent to human existence."[22] She illustrates her understanding of this duality by means of yinyang, the traditional Chinese concept discussed in the preceding chapter: "Gender is not a binary in the sense of 0/1 but a duality in the sense of yinyang. Yin and yang are interpenetrating opposites that constitute each other. There is no yang without yin. . . . They transform into each other. Night becomes day. Day becomes night. They are infinitely divisible. Yin contains yang. Yang contains yin. Men contain femininity, women contain masculinity."[23] Referring to the early literal meaning of yin as the shady side and yang as the sunny side of a hill, she adds:

> There are two genders in the sense of that there are two sides of a mountain. . . . Depending on where the mountain is, the shady side might become the sunny side. There is no shade without light. So, in a sense, the binary is nonbinary. In a way, it would be equally true to say that there is one gender, the human gender, which has been split into two, into three, into many. Because yin and yang are mutually dependent, they are both a duality and a unity: yinyang.[24]

Wynn's language here is just as metaphorical as early Chinese philosophy often is—but her point is conceptually clear: On the one hand, there is a duality between masculine and feminine characteristics or traits; on the other, this duality is also a dynamically interrelated unity. As Scott Barry Kaufman summarizes the matter in *Scientific American*, "a large number of well-done studies" in empirical psychology "painted a rather consistent picture of sex differences in personality that are strikingly consistent across cultures." Kaufman states that "*on average,* males tend to be more dominant, assertive, risk-prone, thrill-seeking, tough-minded, emotionally stable, utilitarian, and open to abstract ideas," whereas "females, *on average,* tend to be more sociable, sensitive, warm, compassionate, polite, anxious, self-doubting, and more open to aesthetics."[25] While the list of academically studied sex and gender differences is almost endless, it is important to emphasize, as Kaufman does, that such differences must not be regarded as defining of any particular individual. He writes, "I can recognize that I am a man who has quite a mix of extremely masculine and extremely feminine personality traits."[26] Something similar can probably be said about most people. Importantly, gender traits are mixed differently in each individual, and no person has a "pure" set of gender traits: the risk-prone may sometimes be risk-averse, and the polite will be impolite on occasion. There is neither a timeless consistency nor an internal cohesion to these traits in a person. What is more, they are not anchored in or owned by any core self—instead they are conditioned epigenetically, hormonally, socially, etc., and change in response to coincidental triggers and circumstances. A person's duality of feminine and masculine traits is not rooted in *the person*, and yet we somewhat overconfidently label them "personality traits" and identify our *selves* with them—as Kaufman does too when he writes, "I *am* a man" who "has" those mixed traits.

One central gender difference is sexual orientation. On average, men are mostly gynephile, i.e., attracted to women, while women are mostly androphile, i.e., attracted to men—for obvious evolutionary reasons. In combination with gender identity, sexual orientation tends to be reified as a central characteristic of the supposed self, especially in the context of contemporary identity politics. But on closer inspection, sexual orientation is, just like gender traits, not an essential characteristic of a core self but contingent on various factors, including cultural practices and prevailing identity technologies.

In Western societies, many sexual practices that used to be shunned as "perversions" are now tolerated and, at times, celebrated. While this is decidedly not the case with pedophilia, it is well-known that sex between teenage boys and older men was both common and socially esteemed in ancient Greece—which is sometimes labeled "the cradle of Western civilization." Plato's works, particularly the *Symposium*, and Greek pictorial art depict such "pederasty" as spiritually valuable and aesthetically beautiful.[27] But men who had sex with boys in ancient Greece did not identify as gay—there wasn't even a proper word for a "homosexual" or "bisexual" person in the language, and there was no concept of "sexual orientation."[28] Depending on social status, having sex with boys, and enjoying it, was part of the sincere enactment of adult male role-identity, and perfectly compatible with being married to and having sex with a woman. Being androphile was not seen as a feminine trait in a man. People identified in completely different ways with sexual practices, gender traits, and sexual orientations in ancient Greece than they are expected to today.

In an article published at NBC News in March 2024, Brooke Sopelsa reports enormous generational differences in sexual orientation in the United States. The headline reads, "Nearly 30% of Gen Z women identify as LGBTQ, Gallup survey finds."[29] Gen Z women (born between 1995 and 2010) are especially likely to identify as bisexual: about 20 percent do so. These numbers contrast with 0.6 percent of baby boomers (born before 1965) who identify as bisexual and approximately 1.5 percent who identify with the broader category of LGBTQ. This phenomenal rise of LGBTQ identity, particularly among women, can hardly be explained as the birth of a rather different kind of self around the turn of the millennium. Instead, it seems obvious that social and cultural changes, together with—as proposed throughout this book—changes in identity technology, lead to the construction of different self-narratives, particularly with regard to gender and sexual orientation.

Whatever was experienced by an adult man having sex with boys in ancient Greece, and whatever is experienced by a bisexual Gen Z woman in today's United States, they made and still make use of socially provided options to construct gender identities for themselves. Unlike in ancient Greece, Gen Z people today often also need to define their sexual orientation in relation to the LGBTQ+ spectrum in addition to their gender. There is no correct, coherent, or historically stable match between biological sex, masculine and feminine personality traits, and the kind of persons with whom one has sex. With regard to both gender and sexual orientation, a sense of coherent self-identity is built on underlying incongruities and social-biological-psychological contingencies.

A SURVIVAL STORY

Natalie Wynn illustrates her argument for gender duality with the notion of yinyang. In Daoist philosophy, yinyang indeed represents the two relational, opposite, complementary, and mutually inclusive moments constituting the ever-continuing reproduction and transformation of life, of the cosmos, or of the Dao. The yinyang horizon can be understood as "gendering" everything that exists: the weather, the seasons, and the movements of the heavenly bodies. All these phenomena have been described as yinyang processes. No matter how attractive one may find such a transhumanist or non-anthropocentric yinyang metaphysics, it is still a metaphysics, and therefore not necessarily the best framework for understanding what gender identity actually is today, or was throughout history. The point of the present book is not to replace a Western binary gender metaphysics with an Eastern dualist one but to move beyond a metaphysical or theological conception of gender altogether.

After two billion years of presexual life, sexual reproduction evolved over a further five hundred million to one billion years, resulting in the emergence of two sexes, commonly called male and female, and relatively rare intersex cases. Gender theologies and metaphysics, however, including the yinyang metaphysics, did not evolve biologically—they are social constructs. Luhmann proposed to label the former (sexual) differentiation between male and female a "classification" and the latter (gender) differentiation a "distinction." Crucially, he pointed out, the latter does not follow from the *Sache selbst*—the thing *itself.* Instead, gender distinctions are made somewhat arbitrarily: "They are constructions of a reality which could be constructed in a completely different way based on completely different distinctions."[30] This is to say, gender metaphysics do not accurately mirror our biology but are socially and historically contingent. This is the case for both Western binary and Eastern duality gender metaphysics—as well as for today's metaphysics of a gendered self. No matter how much we'd like to convince ourselves of a gender metaphysics, the meaning that we ascribe to gender is always socially supplied, by the beliefs, the values, the language, the social structures, the power relations, and the identity technologies that prevail in the society we live in. There is no meaning in sex as the *Sache selbst*—*all* the meaning biology takes on is ascribed to it from the outside. And so, no gender metaphysics ever gets sex "right."

To avoid falling into the trap of merely replacing one gender metaphysics with another, it can be useful to look for some alternative critical—and therapeutic—reflections on gender identity. As noted previously, I read Daoism as a philosophy that teaches us *not how to get gender (metaphysics) right but how to cope with the social regimes that pressure us to take on this mission impossible!*

One major narrative genre in the *Zhuangzi* are the "skill stories" about Daoist practitioners who have extraordinary knacks, typically for rather mundane activities such as training fighting cocks, catching cicadas, or falling off carts when drunk. Some of the stories emphasize not just amazing skills but also the art of *surviving in dangerous situations.* One such survival story is about an unnamed diver who jumps down an enormous waterfall that even fish cannot pass.³¹ Coincidentally, Confucius sees the diver perform his trick and, apparently fearing that the diver may have killed himself, sends out his students to retrieve the body. But the diver emerges completely unharmed, "walking along the bank singing, his hair streaming down his back."³² Totally astonished, Confucius asks him if he has a special *way,* or Dao, to deal with the waters. "No," the diver responds, "I have no Dao." He then adds cryptically, "I started out with the grounding, grew along with the nature of the situation, and finished up with fate." Confucius doesn't understand, and the diver explains: "I was born on land and became comfortable on land; this is the grounding. I grew up with the water and became comfortable in water; this is the nature of the situation. I am how I am without knowing how; this is fate."

There are numerous layers of allegorical meaning to the story. One way of understanding it is via the key metaphor of swimming or diving, which in the original text is *you*—a term that has the broader meaning of (carefree) wandering, or being at ease. The question of how to swim through troubled waters, or of how to maintain one's mental sanity in adverse social circumstances, is a major therapeutic theme in the *Zhuangzi*. Seen in this way, the diver is an allegorical representation of the Daoist art of existential survival.

If the story is read as an existential allegory, the diver's outright rejection of having any Dao can be interpreted as being free from any ideology, any set of dogmatic values, or metaphysics. His extraordinary comfort with where he was born and how he grew up can be regarded as a successful adaptation to the contingencies of life. And his not knowing much about himself can be understood as having a very light sense of self, mirroring his rejection of any dogmatic beliefs. The image of the diver "walking along the bank singing, his hair streaming down his back," metaphorically expresses the relaxation and contentment that allow him to eschew harm.

Given some leeway for philosophical fancy, the allegory of the Daoist diver can also be related to today's discourses on gender identity. Its point would then be, first, to become content with how one is born—that is, with one's biological sex. Second, the task would be to become content with the "nature of the situation" one comes to face—that is, becoming content with the gender identity that must be constructed on top of many underlying contingencies and incongruities. Such contentment, the story would imply, follows from remaining unharmed by the metaphysical, religious, or moralistic dogmas around sex and gender, and from not trying to build an all too rigid sense of a gendered self.

We are not born with a sense of self but establish it over time by means of the identity technologies we apply. This is to say, the self becomes real and true, or "genuine," by being performed and internalized. There is no true (but also no fake) self from the start; rather, it is built through the practice of often rather rigid regimes: sincere commitment to one's roles, or the pursuit of authentic selfhood, or, for that matter, true investment in one's profiles. One's sense of self is typically related to gender and sexuality in one way or another. From a Daoist perspective, surviving all the potential torments created by the regimes that shape our gender identities and sexual orientations is helped by the realization that gender identities and sexual orientations are genuinely pretended.

3

BEYOND THE WEST

From Gender Roles to Profiles

BEFORE AND AFTER AUTHENTICITY

The struggle with authenticity that characterizes debates and confusions about gender identity—such as the quest, described by Miquel Missé, to match one's body with one's "true self"—has been a mostly Western phenomenon. The great philosophers of autonomy and authenticity, from Kant to Sartre, were European, and the shift to a modern world society with its focus on individualism happened in the context of Western industrialization, Western liberalism and capitalism, and Western imperialism and colonialism. But today, the semantics and values of autonomy and authenticity are often understood to be *universally* valid—or, as famously suggested by Francis Fukuyama back in 1992, as marking the "end of history."[1]

Before engaging in a critique of the continuing Western struggle with gender authenticity, I intend to look beyond the Western sphere and discuss conceptions of gender and transgender identity before and after authenticity in Asia and other non-Western places. The purpose is to question the claim to universality of the authenticity paradigm informing current Western "identity politics." Moreover, I want to show that post-authentic practices of gender and transgender have already been emerging in "other" places—which proves that the age of authenticity cannot be regarded as the "end of history."

THE DISSOLUTION OF
THE CHINESE FAMILY

Traditional gender roles were socially and psychologically grounded in the family. Before modernity, growing up in a family, which often encompassed more than two generations, was the global norm. There were different families, of course: large and small, rich and poor, monogamous and polygamous. And there were exceptions: orphans and slaves, for example, often could not live with their families. Notwithstanding this diversity, people commonly grew up with their biological parents in the roles of daughters and sons, and with their sisters and brothers. They then became wives and husbands, mothers and fathers, grandmothers and grandfathers, and so on.

Reflecting a deep cultural concern with relations between family members, the Chinese language has dozens of designations for the various roles a person has in their family. The language distinguishes in great detail between relatives on the mother's and father's side and between older and younger siblings. There are different formal terms for your father's older sister (*gumu* 姑母), your father's younger sister (*gujie* 姑姐), your father's older brother's wife (*bomu* 伯母), your father's younger brother's wife (*shenmu* 婶母), your mother's sister (*yimu* 姨母), and your mother's brother's wife (*jiumu* 舅母)—whereas in English, all of these are referred to as "aunts." When it comes to "cousins" in traditional Chinese terminology, it's even more complicated. This level of distinction resulted in an astoundingly complex network where everyone had a different relation to everyone else and one therefore needed to exercise a wide variety of roles—which were all gendered. The age- and gender-based hierarchical structure of the family imposed an intricate regime of sincerity on everyone. Throughout the course of their lives, people were busy acting and thinking—that is, *identifying* themselves—in line with their numerous gendered roles, from which there was no escape.

In today's China, especially in the huge megacities that contain a total of about one billion people,[2] the traditional family structure is mostly a remnant of the past. China's miraculous economic rise since the late 1970s lifted hundreds of millions of people out of rural poverty and into a new urban middle class. This process and the concurrent "one-child policy," which lasted until 2015,[3] made Chinese families increasingly look like the "standard" small core family known from contemporary Europe and North America: a (heterosexual male-female) couple and one (biological) child. But given recent developments, it seems that the small core family was a mere intermediary stage in a larger historical process leading to the complete dissolution of the traditional extended family. In "What Killed Marriage?," Michael Kwan of the China Europe International Business School writes:

> Official statistics show that the number of registered divorces in China increased from 2.7 million in 2010 to 4.7 million in 2019— up by a whopping 75.5% in a decade. A further look into the divorce/marriage ratio (the number of divorces compared to the number of marriages in a certain region within a given period) reveals an even gloomier picture. *In 2019, China's divorce/marriage ratio was 50.7%, indicating that the number of divorces surpassed half of the number of marriages.* In the same year, Tianjin reported the highest rate (72.5%), followed by the three north-eastern provinces

of Liaoning, Jilin, and Heilongjiang (averaging over 60%). Divorce rates in Beijing, Chongqing, and Shanghai were also close to 60%.[4]

The rapid rise in divorce rates in China, especially in the economically and socially advanced urban areas, is accompanied by an almost equally extreme decline in marriage rates. On the online data platform Statista, Felix Richter reports that "the marriage rate in China dropped to a historic low of 4.8 new marriages per 1,000 people in 2022, down from more than double that a decade earlier."[5] "Young adults in particular are increasingly likely to delay or forgo marriage altogether, breaking away from the longstanding societal pressure to marry early," Richter notes. "While 47% of newly married people in China were 24 or younger in 2005, that number dropped to just 15% in 2022, with nearly 50% of newlyweds older than 30, compared to less than 20% in 2005." Young people in China are often no longer very keen on marrying, and if they do marry, they do so at a much older age than their parents did. On top of this, they are almost incomparably more likely to divorce than their parents or grandparents were. Unsurprisingly, these drastic changes are reflected in a rapidly declining birth rate. According to Richter, "the Chinese birth rate fell to a new low in 2022, resulting in the country's first population decline in 60 years." The fertility rate in China currently stands at approximately 1.7 per woman.[6]

High and steadily increasing levels of divorce, at over 50 percent of the number of marriages, along with significantly decreasing marriage and birth rates means that the "standard" core family of a married couple raising one or two biological children will *not* be the norm in China for long. Instead, children will grow up with single parents, in patchwork families, or in the care of other relatives such as grandparents—or, more likely, in shifting mixtures of various arrangements. Under such circumstances, the traditional Chinese terminology for family members is losing its functionality. What is more, the whole sincerity regime that forced people to strongly identify with gendered family roles throughout their lives is profoundly challenged.

Reports on the rapidly changing data on marriage, divorce, and birth rates in China typically explain that these developments reflect "changing gender roles, increased educational and career opportunities for women and a desire for personal fulfillment outside the confines of a traditional family structure."[7] Echoing this assessment, Michale Kwan writes that in China

> *men and women today stand on a more equal footing when it comes to divorce.* This has much to do with increasing educational levels for women thanks to an improved gender balance in China's higher education system. According to some research, the more educated a woman is, the more likely that she will find a satisfactory partner even after getting a divorce. *Therefore, when confronting marital conflict, well-educated women choose to divorce and seek re-marriage rather than make compromises in their current relationship.*[8]

The breakdown of the traditional Chinese family is both an effect and a cause of the disappearance of traditional gender roles: it's a cyclical pattern. Because of the Chinese one-child policy, many daughters were effectively treated by their parents as sons used to be in the old days: the family concentrated their economic resources on them, they became sole heirs, and they received all possible support (and pressure) regarding their education. This resulted in unprecedented economic power, social status, and independence for many Chinese women, which in turn encouraged many of them not to submit to subordinated female gender roles in their intimate relationships.

In the context of socioeconomic hyper-modernization, the former Chinese one-child policy is currently bringing about, albeit unintentionally, something Marxists had dreamed of back in the nineteenth century: the abolishment of the bourgeois family. Many women in China no longer live *as* women (*funü*) in the earlier sense of living one's whole life *as* wives and *as* daughters. They may remain unmarried or get married for a second or third time. They may have no children or, if they do, they may not live with them on a daily basis. And if they do live with a child, it may not be their biological son or daughter. Instead of identifying primarily with old-fashioned gender roles, many Chinese women are busy building their professional profiles in their careers and curating their evolving personal profiles on social media.

The dissolution of the traditional family in China is happening fast, occurring within just a few generations. China is moving quickly from pre- to postmodern family structures. In the process, it has almost skipped the phase in which the Western-style core family is the common norm. This jump in social "technology" mirrors speedy technological innovation—not many people in China had individual landline phones or desktop computers. China shifted swiftly from having almost no personal communication devices at all to a near-ubiquity of cellphones, laptops, and tablets. What is more, in the realm of identity technologies China took a shortcut from sincerity to profilicity, not spending much time in between with authenticity.

CUTE GENDER

The rather quick transition from pre- to postmodern family structures is not a uniquely Chinese phenomenon. Many countries in East Asia underwent similar developments. A study reports that "in East Asian countries, divorce rates have been rising steadily since 1980," adding that

> substantial increases in divorce rates in East Asian countries signify a significant change in circumstances and attitudes to divorce because, in the past, divorce carried a considerable stigma and the pressure to remain in a disharmonious marriage for "the sake of the children" and also for the sake of appearances and family honor was very strong. It would appear that factors such as increasing economic independence of woman, and the pressures of the big city environments in which an increasing proportion of East Asians live, are influencing divorce trends.[9]

What is more, East Asia also has the highest childlessness levels in the world today. The demographer Tomáš Sobotka points out that the total fertility rate dropped below one child per woman in locations including South Korea, Hong Kong, and Taiwan. He further explains:

> The emergence of very low fertility in East Asia has often been interpreted as a consequence of the rapid postponement of marriage and the rising share of women who do not marry during their reproductive lives. Unlike in other highly developed countries, where the erosion of marriage progressed in tandem with the rise of cohabitation and non-marital childbearing, marriage in East Asia remains closely connected with reproduction. Childbearing outside marriage remains rare, representing only 2%–4% of all children born in South Korea, Japan, Taiwan, and Singapore. . . . Therefore, the rise in permanent singlehood in East Asia is directly mirrored in a rising share of permanently childless women and men.[10]

Clearly, all over East Asia traditional gender roles are losing their meaning when not only divorce but "permanent singlehood and childlessness" become increasingly common. It is impossible for a permanently childless single person to be a "sincere" woman or man in the specific sense of forming one's gendered self in orientation to family roles such as mother, father, husband, or wife. And yet, the gendered self has not disappeared in East Asia. But how is the self gendered *after* the age of sincerity? It seems that the demise of sincere gender identification in Asia coincided with the conspicuous rise of a peculiar virtual gender profile.

I have been teaching for about a decade in Macau, and in my personal experience most students continue to identify themselves in terms of gender. It is common for people in Asia to choose a Western name in addition to their native-language ones. Boys tend to select quite masculine and somewhat "aristocratic" names like Edward or William. Girls, on the other hand, frequently use rather feminine names like Cindy or Fiona. Often, however, students also come up with androgynous names like Winter or Jojo, playfully combining both male and female associations. No matter which genders these names indicate, male, female, or both, they tend to present a sort of cuteness.

Since university teaching today typically also includes online components, students in all of my classes interact with me not just in person but also on educational platforms resembling social media. Here they need to create and curate profiles that might include, on a voluntary basis, a profile picture. It was initially quite surprising to me that most students who added an image to their profile did *not* opt for a photograph of their face. Some chose to do so, but most chose a fantasy picture instead—for instance, a rabbit or a cat or an anime character. In conjunction with their Western names, these images tend to underscore a gender identification by the students, either feminine, masculine, or androgynous. What is more, nearly all of the fantasy profile pictures are *cute*. A typical example of such a cute picture is a Hello Kitty image.

The Hello Kitty character was created about half a century ago. There are Hello Kitty comics, films, and video games, and it appears on clothes, stationery, and almost any other item you may think of. Wikipedia mentions that "in 2008, there were over 50,000 different Hello Kitty branded products."[11] Hello Kitty spread first to other Asian countries, including China, and eventually became a "global megastar."[12] Importantly, Hello Kitty is *the* prototype of the Japanese aesthetic of cuteness, or *kawaii* 可愛い, corresponding to *keai* 可爱 in Chinese, which means literally "loveable" or "lovely." In the wake of Hello Kitty, a cuteness culture or, perhaps better, a "cuteness cult" conquered Asia and from there spread to most of the world. Although *kawaii* cuteness can be traced far back into Japanese history, its contemporary form is quite peculiar. In a hyper-commodified context, it primarily indicates a veneration of cute-looking things manifesting what the ethnologist Konrad Lorenz called the *Kindchenschema*, or "baby schema." The baby schema consists in "a set of infantile physical features such as the large head, round face and big eyes that is perceived as cute and motivates caretaking behavior in other individuals, with the evolutionary function of enhancing offspring survival."[13] As with Hello Kitty, *kawaii* aesthetics often project the baby schema onto images of cats, dogs, rabbits, or other animals that lend themselves to cute anthropomorphized representations. Arguably, the current cat craze—a global phenomenon, but reigning supreme in East Asia, in which the felines are adored as pets and featured on social media in billions of videos, GIFs, and memes—is an extension of the *kawaii* wave.

From the start, Hello Kitty, and contemporary *kawaii* culture generally, has been gendered. Hello Kitty is a girlish figure and was initially created for and marketed "as a character that would appeal to pre-teen girls."[14] Girls can see themselves in the character and identify with its ideal of "girlish cuteness." Moreover, in line with Lorenz's understanding of the "baby schema," it also appeals to *mothering* instincts and the desire to take care of something perceived as cute. Hello Kitty represents a "Japanese femininity" that, as Natalia Konstantinovskaia points out, is "frequently associated with the notion of *kawaii*."[15] Referring to some empirical studies, Konstantinovskaia states that "from early childhood, Japanese people are socialized into the expectation that women must be *kawaii*" and that *kawaii* "is a highly valued attribute associated with Japanese women across age groups, yet connected with innocence and childishness."[16]

Although born female, Japanese *kawaii* soon transcended its confinement to this gender alone. In an article titled "In Japan, Cute Conquers All," published in 2002 by the business news agency Bloomberg, Brian Bremner insisted that both men and women are "hooked on cuteness." Twenty-three years later, in 2025, cuteness has a firm grip on all genders in most parts of Asia, if not the world. The global success of Korean boy bands, for instance, manifests the rise of cuteness beyond the female gender. In a recent monograph, *The Power of Cute*, the British philosopher Simon May maintains that "the cute are seldom exclusively masculine or feminine, but rather possess features of both genders, as they are traditionally conceived, especially facial features."[17] According to May, "adult/child, knowing/ naive, feminine/masculine, good/bad, knowable/ unknowable— the sharpness of these dichotomies breaks down under the aspect of Cute. Perhaps this is why cute objects so often lack clear identities in respect of gender, morality, knowability, age, and indeed ethnicity."[18] Today, *kawaii*/cute is no longer mainly female; it can also be male or transgender. In East Asia today, many young people no longer desire to marry and quite frequently remain childless. But on their profiles, they represent themselves using Hello Kitty or other cute names and images. For them, gender is no longer a role but, via cuteness and the baby schema, still often a crucial part of their profiles.

May dedicates a whole chapter of his monograph to establishing a firm distinction between the "neighboring concepts" of cute and kitsch.[19] He finds multiple differences between them. For instance, cute "can be uncanny" or "radical, inventive, and shocking," whereas kitsch is "conventional."[20] Moreover, kitsch "seeks to conjure a world that is only safe, solid, and uplifting. And to that extent, kitsch portrays a fake world and Cute a truer one."[21] In short, for May kitsch is aesthetically and intellectually worse than cute. His rejection of kitsch as "conventional" and "fake," however, also suggests another distinction between the two categories: kitsch is a Western concept evoking a rejection of inauthenticity, while *kawaii* is Asian and not so much concerned with the authenticity–inauthenticity distinction—it is just cute.

Kawaii, the East Asian contemporary cuteness that spread globally, is, from the theoretical perspective of this book, not inauthentic but non-authentic. Its paradigmatic representative, Hello Kitty, is unburdened by the struggles and paradoxes of authenticity. Along with uncountable other *kawaii* symbols, it helps facilitate the post-sincere reemergence of gender as *profile*. By identifying with *kawaii* imagery, young people in Asia can project their gender identity beyond traditional gender roles or any (Western) claim to "authenticity." One can be *kawaii* in a feminine, masculine, or androgynous fashion. And in any case, it is a clearly curated and openly virtual—that is, a playful (and genuinely pretended)—gender identity.

BETWEEN SINCERITY
AND PROFILICITY

Of course, there is more to gender identity in East Asia than cute profile pictures. Nevertheless, being cute or, relatedly, looking pretty seems to play an important part in making one's gender identity *genuine* both to oneself and to others—in a social context where gender identity is rooted neither in the traditional family roles of the past nor in a supposedly "true self," as stipulated by the authenticity semantics still characterizing present gender discourses in the West.

In a conversation with Fa, a 32-year-old transgender woman from Taiwan, German interviewer Flemming Hansen (also 32 years old, and a friend of Fa) poses questions that reflect the quest for the "true self" in one's gender.[22] Hansen asks: "Do you think your romantic partners strongly fantasized about you as a sexual object . . . before *regarding you as a person*?" and, eventually, "Did the *recognition* by others help you *accepting yourself*?" (my emphases). Interestingly enough, however, the Taiwanese transgender woman does not follow the leads by the Western questioner. Instead of describing the journey toward her new gender in terms of paradigmatic authenticity, as a struggle for recognition of her gendered self, she recollects how she was perceived as pretty. In response to the question about "accepting herself," she says:

> You know what? I don't care. . . . What I mean by "I don't care" is, I kind of don't overthink it when they say, "Oh, you look so

pretty." . . . I got positive feedback from what I did. I look after my hair. I look after my nails. . . . I think they obviously . . . feel "That's great, you've been changed, and you are very pretty, and you have a very good sense of taste, and you dress up very well, and you are pretty." I think they just say the facts because they really think "Your hair is amazing," and not . . ."Oh, you were a man, and now you are trying hard to be a woman, so your hair looks amazing, so that's amazing." No, I think they genuinely think, "Oh, wow, your hair looks so pretty." I don't even care, or I don't even realize, or I don't even remember. . . . You know what I am saying? . . . And that's what I want to do in my whole life.

It seems what Fa "doesn't care" about or, more exactly, doesn't want to "overthink" is whether she is, in the sense of how this term is used in this book, "authentically" a woman. She believes in her femininity because she believes in the validation by the people she interacts with—and why shouldn't she? Her concern is precisely *not* the elusive, metaphysical inner "soul" whose supposed gender others need to acknowledge—and neither, of course, is her concern to be seen as a devoted housewife or obedient daughter. Instead, she wishes to be seen as a *pretty woman*.

Fa is forthcoming about being focused on curating her intended gendered profile rather than on becoming who she supposedly "is." Correcting herself, she says, "I am, ahem, I *describe myself* [my emphasis] as a transgender woman," and then adds, "It's a journey, who I want to be, what kind of body I want to live in." She embarked on this journey in great part by taking good care of her looks. Once those with whom she interacts wholeheartedly embrace this profile, as proven by their feedback and behavior toward her, her new gender identity is validated. And that's what she wants to do throughout her whole life: be truly invested in a gendered profile that others genuinely appreciate.

Gender and transgender identity in East Asia, often via cuteness or prettiness, is increasingly profilic. But the receding regime of sincerity has by no means vanished. Given that sincerity and profilicity are both focused on social validation, reputation, and peer feedback as opposed to being oriented toward the inner self, they are arguably less antagonistic to one another than each is to authenticity. But even if the direct transition from sincerity to profilicity is smoother than the detour via authenticity, it is certainly not without conflicts.

When the interviewer asks Fa about her experience of coming out as transgender, she talks about the reactions of her family members. Her parents, she says, were at the outset "not so sure" and "not supportive." Her cousins, however, were "very supportive," and her brother switched "straight away" to addressing her as "sister." Maintaining close family relationships, both on emotional and social levels, was a crucial concern for her during her transition. She knew that ceasing to identify *as a son* was in clear violation of the gender role expectations of the traditional family. Yet it was very important for her to maintain her role *of a child* to her parents and *of a sibling* to her brother, notwithstanding the change in her gender profile.

From an authenticity perspective, the aim of the "self-realization" of the individual must trump all other concerns and must be pursued if necessary, *against* traditional role expectations in the family. Fa, however, was keen to maintain her sincere role identities while changing her gender profile. When trying to reconcile her sincere and profilic identities with one another, insisting on her authentic selfhood was not an issue to "care about" or "overthink" too much.

In an act available on YouTube, the Asian American stand-up comedian Irene Tu introduces herself like this: "Hi everyone, I'm Irene, my pronouns are she/her [pause]. Yeah, I know I have big 'they' energy [laughter from the audience]."[23] Referring to her androgynous looks, she continues: "Everyone assumes that I am nonbinary, which is what I'm not [laughter]. Yeah, I gotta fight back somehow, right? Yeah, no, I . . . probably . . . am [laughter]." Gender identity today is often no longer self-evident—unlike what was expected in sincerity cultures—and leaves lots of room for ambiguity. And yet, the "correct" use of gendered pronouns can be considered a most serious issue, especially among the LGBTQ+ community to which Tu belongs. Self-ironically, Tu makes fun of the attempt at getting (her own) gender right.

Jokingly, she explains her choice, to identify as a lesbian woman rather than nonbinary, as a branding decision: "I just feel if I still identify as a girl, I am like a cool girl. You know, I am a lesbian who skateboards—that's cool. Yeah, otherwise, I'm just a really boring nonbinary person [laughter]. Okay, like my hair is one color, I don't have any tattoos or piercings, and I think monogamy is okay [laughter]. It's not a good look for the brand, alright [laughter]." Lesbians, she implies, are commonly seen as more "standard" people. Therefore, as a lesbian, she can be considered "interesting" by virtue of being a skateboarder. If she identified as nonbinary, the bar for coolness would be much higher and she wouldn't reach it given her conventional looks and opinions.

Later in her act, Tu mentions that her parents are immigrants from Asia who "came to this country with no money." Alluding to conservative sincerity values associated with Asian people, she points out, "I can't come out to them as having no gender [laughter]. I would be disowned, okay [laughter]." Musing on what would happen if she told her parents she was nonbinary, she imagines them responding: "We don't care, just pick one [laughter]. Ya, be a girl, be a boy [pause]. Honestly, we would prefer boy [laughter]." Tu then explains this presumed preference: "That way we can brag to our friends [laughter], yeah, like, 'Our son is a comedian.' I don't know, it's still better than 'Our daughter is a doctor,' you know [laughter]."

Tu satirically contrasts the traditional sincerity perspective on gender—her parents' supposed preference for a son over a daughter—with the profilic approach to gender, which, as she comically implies, is present in the LGBTQ+ community. What counts most for her parents whose origins are Asian is that they can brag to their friends—that is, their personally known peers—about having a son. In a profilicity approach to gender, however, gender needs to be displayed in a cool way—that is, in a way "good for the brand" in the eyes of a general peer group.

To be sure, the imagined pragmatic reaction of Tu's parents to her coming out is humorously twisted. In reality, they would probably not be so unfazed. Tu admits as much: "Don't worry guys, I made it up. Okay, I don't even talk to my dad [laughter]." Still, Tu's joke about her parents "supporting" her becoming a son reveals a compatibility between the sincere and the profilic approaches to gender. In both cases, the performance aspect and peer validation are crucial.

AGAINST THE INDIVIDUALISM VS. COLLECTIVISM FRAMEWORK

Perceived differences between the West and the East or, even more broadly, between the West and the non-West, have been explained in terms of a distinction between individualist and collectivist cultures. Such a framework characterizes a large portion of "Oriental" studies since the nineteenth century as well as various "self-Orientalizations" in the non-West, such as the discourse on "Asian values."[24] One prominent proponent of this framework was the Dutch social psychologist and management researcher Geert Hofstede (1928–2020), who applied it in his book *Culture's Consequences: Comparing Values, Behaviors, Institutions, and Organizations Across Nations*, first published in 1981.[25] Hofstede's distinction between individualism and collectivism is problematic for numerous reasons.

First, the core notion of distinct cultures underlying his theory is highly unspecific. What exactly is a culture? What are its historical, geographical, or ethnic boundaries?

Second, it is problematic to suggest, as the title of Hofstede's book does, that cultures define different "nations" that can then be scientifically compared to one another.

Third, it is questionable whether Western "culture" is indeed well described as "individualistic." While the age of authenticity has certainly developed a very elaborate individualist semantics that strongly inform politics, law, media, science, and more, and that guide social and personal self-descriptions, it is important to differentiate between these narratives and reality. The age of authenticity and its pursuit of originality and uniqueness are paradoxical. This pursuit dialectically produces its opposite: non-originality and sameness. In practice, individualism tends to grossly overestimate its own individuality. The "sovereign individual" at the center of individualism is an idea—not an empirical reality.

Fourth, individualism and the age of authenticity are historically recent phenomena, dating back to the beginnings of modernity. They characterize not the "West" or its "culture" but rather a specific historical period. Before modernity, "Western culture" was hardly individualistic.

Fifth, the characterization of Asian or Chinese "culture" as "collectivist" is misleading. While regimes of sincerity indeed emphasize role-relationships that can exist only in a group—thereby establishing a relational sense of self—the resulting peer groups or networks are not necessarily best described as "collective." Some anecdotal evidence supporting this is provided by my friend and colleague Markus Heidingsfelder, who teaches in Zhuhai, China. Markus asked a local taxi driver why the Chinese male soccer team has been so notoriously unsuccessful. The answer: "Because we Chinese are not good at teamwork." Chinese and other sincerity-based peer groups, as exemplified by the traditional extended family, are characterized by hierarchical relationships that produce contradictory effects of solidarity, competition, discrimination, etc., within the group. These result not just in "collectivity" but also in tensions, divisions, and exclusions.

Sixth, peer relations under conditions of sincerity are limited to present peers. Peer groups (the Asian crime organizations called "triads," for example) often have conflicting interests. They may oppose one another, and that makes "collective" cooperation between groups, on a larger scale, difficult if not impossible.

Seventh, missing from the dualistic distinction between individualism and collectivism is a third element, the contemporary post-authentic and post-individualist condition. Even if premodernity could be described as collectivist, and modernity as individualist, what about postmodernity?

The rise of profilicity makes the culturalist distinction between individualism and collectivism increasingly obsolete. The distinction is of especially little use regarding questions of identity, gender, and sexuality. Better suited to address such questions, both generally and from an East–West comparative angle, is, arguably, the theoretical framework of sincerity, authenticity, and profilicity.

THIRD GENDERS

In an online article provocatively titled "The sex binary is not a 'Western construct,' gender identity is," L. Beatrice, who introduces herself as "a feminist lawyer from the South of India who specialized in international human rights law and with particular expertise in laws and procedures against sexual violence," argues vigorously against what she calls "the coopting and misrepresentation of sexual minorities and gender non-conforming people in Eastern and Southern cultures" in current Western discourses about (trans-)gender identity.[26] Beatrice argues from a traditional feminist position, and her main intention is to counter the claim by some transgender activists "that older cultures recognized the authenticity of 'transgender people'" and to counter the notion that transgender people can be regarded as contemporary forms of traditional non-Western third genders. For an example, she points to a piece by Amrou Al-Kadhi in the online edition of the *Independent*. There, Al-Kadhi claims that "British colonists exported with them strict binary classifications of sex" and that therefore the idea of a clear distinction, rather than fluidity, between the two sexes is firmly tied into "white supremacy."[27] Al-Kadhi then lists "the transgender Hijra people of India" and "the transgender Two-Spirit traditions" among indigenous people in the Americas as victims of a transphobic white supremacy.

According to Beatrice, however, non-Western sexual minorities and gender-nonconforming people such as the hijra, the two-spirit people, or the khawaja sira in Pakistan should not be labeled "transgender." Beatrice argues that these communities neither questioned basic differences between the two sexes, male and female, nor stipulated "that men could literally *be* female."[28] For Beatrice, current transgender advocates tend to be "Westerncentric," and their attempt to claim universality by associating themselves with non-Western traditions betrays not only historical blindness but runs the risk of ending up in a new ideological colonialism where foreign "cultural identities" are "being erased and misunderstood."

Informing Beatrice's piece are the fierce and sometimes overly polemic debates between transgender activists and traditional feminists, who are sometimes dismissed as TERFs (trans-exclusive radical feminists). However, Beatrice's subtle analysis of the distinction between traditional "gender non-conforming communities," as she describes them, and contemporary transgender people is both pertinent and noteworthy. In effect, this distinction amounts to the difference between conceiving of transgender as neither male nor female and defining it as transitioning from one gender to another supposedly more "correct" one. This difference is indeed crucial, and it has a lot to do with the difference between gender under conditions of sincerity and gender under conditions of profilicity. Beatrice's critical analysis of the cultural appropriation of non-Western gender-nonconforming communities by some of today's transgender advocates can be helpful to the work of better understanding the distinction between gender as role and gender as profile.

Beatrice's short piece deals first, and most extensively, with the Indian hijras. "Hijra" is a Hindi language term and refers to "third gender," or, as Beatrice prefers to say, "third sex" communities. Like the khawaja sira in Pakistan, hijra are marginal, discriminated against, and often poor. They often are sex workers, performers, or beggars and/or deliver religious and ritual services. According to Beatrice, "most are men who undergo voluntary castration and penectomy and consider themselves to be sexually impotent." However, the term is not very precise and, as Beatrice says, can "lump in together" a "variety of communities." Hijra "have been described or classed in wildly different ways," and the term has been used to designate "different groups, including eunuchs, transvestites, people with ambiguous genitalia, or sexually 'ambivalent' men who dress up as women."[29]

Despite this lack of terminological precision, it seems clear that hijras typically "see themselves as 'neither man nor woman,'"—which is also the title of a 1990 monograph on them by Serena Nanda.[30] As Renate Syed explains, "Hijṛās consider themselves as neither man nor woman, *na mard, na aurat*, since ancient times, and as the 'third gender,' *tīsrī jins*." Accordingly, "there is no 'Trans-ing' at all. Hijṛās are displaying, to speak in Indian terms, 'hijra-ing' or 'thirdgendering,' and not 'male-femaling.'"[31] Syed further explains that the "third gender" was "considered a biological sex which was acquired at the moment of conception and therefore unchangeable; thirdgender persons were believed to be created by nature and therefore innocent of their biological state. They still suffered discrimination; society treated them highly ambivalent[ly], feared, pitied, shunned and ridiculed them." Importantly, "they had to leave their families, created a 'third world' to live in. They succeeded in creating an everlasting side-culture . . .; they formulated a code of conduct, a codex of rules, a value system, religion, rites and regulations, created constructions of body and sexuality and found a niche of survival in a mostly neglecting if not hostile environment." In this niche, they "organized themselves in *khandans*, families, and *ghārānas*, clans, with a *guru* at the top of the hierarchical family-order."[32]

In opposition to muddling hijras together with all other transgender people, Indian transgender activist Reshma Prasad insists that "Hijras are a type of transgender, but the vast majority of transgender people are not Hijras." He elaborates: "I am not a Hijra. I do not live in a community and under the orders of a guru. I do not sing and dance and ask for alms. And I have a right to be upset when I am called a Hijra or confused with a Hijra, and when a Hijra wants to elbow me out and capture a space meant for me."[33]

The kathoeys in Thailand are another Asian third gender group. Whereas the khawaja sira and the hijra are regarded as divinely created in Islamic and Hindu contexts, respectively, the kathoeys emerged within the framework of a Buddhist belief system.[34] In all three cases, the group in question consists mostly of feminine, androphilic biological males—which is also expressed in the colloquial English expression for kathoey, "ladyboy." According to Marie-Thérèse Claes, "the Thai kathoey are traditionally male born. They portray themselves as women and live, in many ways, like them";[35] they "often come to a realisation that they want to live life as a *phuying prahphet song*, second kind of woman, very early in life," when they are in their teens or earlier.[36] Moreover, like the khawaja sira and the hijras, the kathoeys, too, are socially marginalized and often work in entertainment, in the sex industry, or as ritual performers. Claes explains: "Two species of kathoey co-exist: the traditional kathoey of rural Siam, especially in the north and north-east, and the modern day kathoey cabaret performer of the tourist cities, especially in Bangkok and in Pattaya. The old, rural tradition still flourishes; kathoey beauty contests are staged at fairs and carnivals like the Lamphun Lamyai Festival in August, or the Phuket Vegetarian Festival each September."[37]

Further southeast, yet more third gender traditions exist. In Samoa, there are the "Fa'afafine," which, as L. Beatrice says, "translates as 'in the manner of a woman.'"[38] They "are Samoan biological males who behave in a range of feminine-gendered ways, and have been an integrated part of Samoan communities for centuries." Being a Fa'afafine "is mostly about taking on the tasks of women or acting feminine, not necessarily bodily modification or castration, like the Hijra."[39] In Australia, Aboriginal "sistergirls describe themselves as being born biologically male, but are observed to behave in feminine ways, and so surrounding society treats them as having to fulfill the roles and tasks of girls and women, performing women's dancing, ceremony, and other tasks. Personal accounts reveal that they live in the role of women, hunting, sitting, and talking with women."[40]

Various third gender groups are also known among North American indigenous communities: the so-called two-spirit people. According to Deirdre Bell, the Lakota, a part of the larger Sioux nation, "have a longstanding tradition of two-spirit people, documented as far back as the written record goes. Among the Lakota, polygyny was accepted, and gender roles were extremely clearly established for boys and girls from an extremely early age. . . . The Lakota two-spirit people are never born women. Almost all of them, historically, have been men." In this case, as in the previously discussed cases from Asia, the third gender community is constituted by feminine men who take on social roles akin to those of women. Deirdre Bell speculates on the reason for this phenomenon among the Lakota, "Let me postulate a . . . theory: that it's men in power who impose gender roles, and that Lakota men's patriarchal society had to have somewhere to put 'men who don't "act like" men' because of male gender policing. Lakota people put two-spirit men in the part of the camp where women and children lived, which was generally not as well cared for and considered not as prestigious because of the patriarchal way that they lived."[41] Whether or not this speculation is correct, it seems that in Asia and among North American indigenous cultures, third genders were typically, though not exclusively, restricted to "effeminate" biological males. Bell ascribes this peculiar gender imbalance in the sphere of third genders to the generally patriarchic conditions under which they existed: "That's something men do for men, because just by dint of having a penis, gender nonconforming men deserved to be able to have their own group and identity. . . . You see this in large numbers of patriarchal American Indian cultures: societies where there's a firmly established 'third' gender that men can elect to participate in (sometimes as older people, sometimes from an early age), while women's gender roles are firmly entrenched and allow for little variance."[42]

The hypothesis that masculine men among the Lakota people intentionally created a third gender both to accommodate and marginalize men who were more feminine is guesswork and in need of further substantiation. And yet, all the abovementioned third genders were embedded in patriarchal societies. This fact poses a serious challenge to any attempt to idealize traditional third genders as examples of "gender equality" in native societies, or to cite them as cases in point for a gender-affirming attitude to transgender. Crucially, all those third genders functioned not in opposition to but as an extension of the strict hierarchies between the two genders, male and female, and their respective role assignments in those societies.

However, not all traditional third genders in patriarchal societies were tailored to male-born individuals with feminine traits—and not all of them were "non-Western." The present book is written in Belgrade, Serbia. A few hundred kilometers further south, some "Balkan sworn virgins" are still alive, mostly in remote rural regions. In recent years, they attracted the attention of major Western media outlets. A feature article by Andrew Higgins in August 2021 in the *New York Times* includes photos of these women and reports on their views and experiences.[43] One is Gjystina Grishaj, who was in her late fifties and is also portrayed in both video and text in a December 2022 piece, by Tui McLean for the BBC, with the somewhat sensationalist title "The Last of Albania's Sworn Virgins."[44] According to this piece, "it is estimated that there are only 12 burrneshat remaining in Northern Albania and Kosovo." *Burrnesha* is an Albanian term, meaning literally, as the *New York Times* feature indicates, "female-men."

As Higgins, explains, the sworn virgins took "an oath of lifelong celibacy" that enabled them to "enjoy male privileges, like the right to make family decisions, smoke, drink and go out alone." In effect, a burrnesha lived the life of a single man and could fill masculine roles such as "breadwinner" of the family. There were various reasons for becoming a burrnesha. Families might have had no male heir owing to the historical prevalence of blood feuds, and may therefore have assigned the role of son to one of their daughters. In this way, they could inherit property—which normally was not possible for women according to the local Kanun, the traditional Albanian legal, ritual, and moral code—and could eventually become the head of the household, claiming its possessions and rights in the community. Becoming a sworn virgin was also an option for women who rejected a forcibly arranged marriage, or who wished "to enjoy freedoms only men could experience" and, like Gjystina Grishaj, did not "like cooking, ironing clothes or 'doing any of the things that women do.'"[45] Others, like "Diana Rakipi, 66, a burrnesha in the coastal city of Durres," as Higgins reports, "always felt like a man, even as a boy."[46]

Despite her stated masculine self-perception and choice to become a "female-man," Diana Rakipi does not identify as a man and strongly rejects gender-affirmative medical intervention. She "snorted with contempt when asked about people who undergo transition surgery. 'It is not normal,' she said. 'If God made you a woman, you are a woman.'"[47] Gjystina Grishaj expresses the same seemingly paradoxical ambiguity toward her gender. She "adopted a male nickname—Duni" and yet not only "does not consider herself transgender" but "shares the strongly transphobic and homophobic views that are prevalent in Albania."[48] Echoing Rakipi's opinion on sexual transitioning, she believes that "altering the body goes 'against God's will' " and that "people 'should be put in jail for doing so.' "[49] She adds: "I have not lived as a burrnesha because I want to be a man in any physical way. I have done this because I want to take on the role played by men and to get the respect of a man." She is "a man in my spirit," she asserts, "but having male genitals is not what makes you a man."[50] The clear distinction that both Rakipi and Grishaj make between their sex and their gender, not on a conceptual or terminological level but in a practical way, is arguably representative of many other sworn virgins in their culture. They fully embrace their burrnesha identities in terms of gender as "female-men" while rejecting any suggestion that they are transgender in the sense of being born into the "wrong body" or with the wrong biology. They neither desire sex changes nor claim that they are men— they are burrneshat.

Both the *New York Times* feature and the BBC piece on the sworn virgins point out that this third gender is firmly embedded in the patriarchal role divisions in traditional Balkan societies. "Duni was not striking at conventional gender norms but submitting to them," Andrew Higgins concludes.[51] Furthermore, he refers to the local ethnographer Gjok Luli, who also stresses that the rigid role framework within which the gender change of the sworn virgins takes place remains fully intact. Becoming a burrnesha is "an escape from the role given to women." But, on the other hand, this "escape" from one role results only in the lifelong submission to another role that is just as binding. Luli compares a burrnesha to a "woman who decides to become a nun," adding that "it is the same kind of devotion, only to the family instead of God."[52] Luli's assessment is fully confirmed by Gjystina Grishaj, quoted as saying in the BBC piece: "There are many unmarried people in the world, but they are not burrneshat. A burrnesha is dedicated only to her family, to work, to live, to preserve her purity."[53] In the case of the sworn virgins, remaining single is by no means a rejection of traditionally gendered family roles; to the contrary, a burrnesha is a third gendered role—or "gender identity," if you will—that thoroughly affirms the patriarchal social structures built on the "sex binary."

Remarkably different from current transgender discourses that describe the life of a transgender person as a journey that can fluidly move between genders, Grishaj insists otherwise: "I can't resign from the role I have chosen. I took an oath to my family. This is a path you cannot go back on."[54] She is fully aware that her gender role has been "chosen" by herself, but in this case, "choosing" does not imply open-ended "free will"; it means instead that precisely because one's gender role was one's own choice, one cannot ever "self-determine" one's gender again if one has second thoughts about it.

Grishaj's notion of choice is strikingly different from the modern notion of individual autonomy. Under a regime of sincerity, a role that one chooses—including, if a society offers this option, a gender role—is no less binding than the "common" roles one is born into. If anything, a sincerely self-chosen gender role is *more* binding and demanding than one assigned at birth. In sincerity, identity is formed by an intense behavioral and psychological commitment to roles. Here the foothold for orientation lies in the roles and not, as the age of authenticity assumes, in the self. The role is, so to speak, the source of authority. Under conditions of authenticity, this changes, and the role loses its authority. In authenticity, *choice* must always be a choice for *oneself*—and not for the role that is considered an arbitrary mask externally imposed on the self, especially if it is a traditional gender role. The authentic individual chooses *not* to be identified by any gender role. Today, under conditions of profilicity, "choice" is changing its meaning once more. Here, gender can become a foothold for self-identification again—but in the forms of chosen gender profiles rather than roles. Unlike roles, profiles are highly dynamic and "fluid," owing to their emergence out of social-validation feedback loops. As stipulated in the German bill on the self-determination of gender (further discussed in the following chapter), a person can choose their gender identity once a year. Cleary, this concept of gender choice has little in common with Grishaj's decision to become a burrnesha.

This short overview of various traditional third genders, from the hijra in Asia to the two-spirit people among the Lakota in North America to the sworn virgins in Europe, supports L. Beatrice's claim that the sex binary is not a Western invention. More precisely, it supports the claim that many forms of third gender in traditional societies do not subvert or challenge the basic assumption that there are two "normal" sexes, male and female. That society must be ordered on the basis of rather strict role divisions and hierarchies between them was accepted in the contexts in which these forms of third gender emerged. Most traditional societies were patriarchal, and within their patriarchal structures some allowed for a third, "nonnormal" gender. This third gender, however, was not open to anybody who might regard themselves as "gender diverse" or "transgender" but rather was typically set up either as a "female-like" gender for biological males (e.g., the hijra) or a "male-like" gender for biological females (like the burrneshat). Importantly, these third genders were regulated just as strongly by social conventions, or regimes of sincerity, as were the other two genders. In short, the third gender was an extension of male and female gender roles to people of the respective other sex, with the crucial exception that they couldn't have "normal" families or procreate. Third genders consisted either in roles enabling men to live in a feminine way, but not as wives or mothers, or in roles enabling women to live in a masculine way, but not as husbands or fathers.

Access to a third gender often depended on personal choice—but the choice needed to be sincere, and not authentic or profilic. Once a hijra or sworn virgin, always a hijra or sworn virgin. For traditional third genders as much as for the two others, identity building was based on lifelong commitment to one's roles rather than on pursuing originality or curating a profile. Seen from this perspective, it is entirely understandable that a burrnesha rejects any association with today's transgender. The difference in identity technology between sincerity and profilicity is so pronounced that it outweighs by far the similarity between being a sexual minority and a gender-nonconforming person.

FOOTBINDING AND MUTILATION-IMPROVEMENT

Personal commitment to a third gender identity can be so radical that it includes acts of bodily self-mutilation. Importantly, however, this mutilation is not perceived as such but, on the contrary, as a bodily improvement or correction by a person who undergoes it not only voluntarily but, possibly, even happily. As mentioned, some hijra have their penises excised. A study published online by Harvard Divinity School explains: "Many [hijra], but not all, choose to undergo a castration ceremony, removing their male genitalia as an offering to Hindu goddess Bahuchara Mata."[55] Here, the ritual commitment to a gender identity in the form of bodily mutilation-improvement is at the same time also a commitment to the person's religious identity. It can be assumed that a hijra experiences this double commitment, and the castration ceremony that expresses it, as a blissful affirmation of their selfhood.

The pursuit of a sincere gender identity by means of a paradoxical mutilation-improvement of the body is not limited to third genders. One of the most widely known traditional forms of gender identity commitment expressed by means of inflicting pain on the body and diminishing its functions was female footbinding in China. The practice probably goes back to the tenth century CE, became common in the twelfth century, and lasted until it was socially, politically, and legally opposed in modern China toward the end of and, especially, after the fall of the last imperial dynasty in 1912.[56]

To be effective, footbinding commonly started at a preteen age. Accordingly, it was usually not a matter of "informed choice" but a decision made for the female child by the patriarchally organized family into which she was born. In her monograph *Aching for Beauty: Footbinding in China*, Wang Ping writes, "Little girls were initiated into the binding between the ages of five and seven, when their bones were still flexible . . . and their minds mature enough . . . to understand the importance of this bodily discipline," which subjected them to a long period of intense physical pain.[57] The process involves not only binding but also the breaking of bones in the toes and other parts of the child's foot. Bleeding and rotting of flesh occurred, which often caused infections.[58] The aim was to minimize the size of the feet and to shape them in the form of an arch.

As Dorothy Ko points out in her self-labeled "revisionist history of footbinding," titled *Cinderella's Sisters*, "there is not one footbinding but many," because "the practice, its rationale, and its reception changed over time during its almost millennium-long spread across class and geographical boundaries."[59] Over centuries, footbinding spread from northern to southern China, from the upper classes to wider segments of the population, and the feet became increasingly smaller and more arched. The practice reached its peak between the seventeenth and nineteenth centuries, but regional differences remained, and it was uncommon among ethnic minorities.[60] Notwithstanding these differences, as Wang states, footbinding was generally "accepted by society as a symbol for feminine beauty, hierarchy, and morality."[61] It was regarded as erotic and attractive, as classy and noble, and as cultured and refined. Accordingly, for upper-class women footbinding could be a "marker of their hierarchy," and for lower-class women it could increase their value as potential brides, or as female entertainers, thereby giving them "an opportunity to move upward in the marriage and service market."[62] And, most obviously, it was a marker of gender identity: it was exclusively female.

Wang explains that mothers usually took care of the footbinding process of their daughters. Thereby, Wang suggests, a strong bond was established that constituted the message of footbinding: "a truly loving mother must teach her daughter how to endure pain physically, emotionally, and mentally. Such love mixed and reinforced with unspeakable pain and violence is . . . the secret language/knowledge . . . that teaches the daughter about the mapping and discipline of the female body in a patriarchal environment, and that prepares her for her sexuality, marriage, reproduction, motherhood."[63] The year-long ordeal imposed by the mother on the daughter powerfully initiated her into her roles in the patriarchal society. More than just a physical mutilation, it was also an "improvement" of her looks and moral and social prestige. Perhaps most importantly, it intensified the internalization of her gender roles. It was an application of a social and psychological identity technology.

With her "revisionist history of footbinding," Dorothy Ko—rather than merely participating in the common denouncing of footbinding—wishes to show that "the reality of the practice" should not be reduced to "the screams and the tears on a girl's first day of binding." Instead, Ko seeks "to locate the woman's agency and subjectivity not only in the world that the pain destroyed, but also in the subsequent unfolding and creation of meanings: for each woman, footbinding was an ongoing process, just as each body was located in a specific time and place."[64] Ko's focus on "the woman's agency and subjectivity" reproduces the prevalent language of the age of authenticity. It presumes the pursuit of originality, an identity technology that differs greatly from the commitment to roles. It is questionable, though, if such a pursuit can indeed be projected onto a preteen girl in premodern China on her "first day of biding."

In historical literary descriptions of women engaging in footbinding, Ko detects "the female delight in her own ability to remake her body" so that "a sense of agency" is "felt by the woman in the process of binding."[65] It is entirely conceivable—and, for the sake of their psychological well-being, to be hoped for—that the women who underwent the mutilation of their feet as children would eventually not just accept but welcome it as a form of self-improvement. After all, this is what society had suggested to them: that footbinding would make not just their feet and their body but their whole person more valuable *as women*. And it is of course true that, although the binding was, at the outset, done to young girls by their mothers, they eventually did it by themselves once they had grown up—and at that stage it could be perceived as an expression of "agency" or "subjectivity." However, this kind of agency or subjectivity is clearly not authentic—it is an agency based on the internalization of and the sincere commitment to the female role identity that had defined the meaning of footbinding in the first place.

Ko finds "agency" and "subjectivity" in footbinding in "the assiduous maintenance and care a Chinese woman lavished on her feet every day for the rest of her life" after the practice was imposed on her.[66] Yes, but what better choice did a woman have "for the rest of her life," once her mother had started binding her feet, other than attending to them with "assiduous mainte-nance and care"? It seems obvious that the best social and psy-chological option for her was to eventually *identify* with this choice and make it her own by dedicating herself wholly to it. This is "agency" and "subjectivity" within the bounds of a regime of sincerity—a regime that, in this case, is enforced through a paradoxical bodily self-mutilation-improvement.

Voluntary castration by hijra and footbinding enforced among Chinese girls are two cases of bodily mutilation-improvement in the service of sincere gender identity—transgender in the first instance, and cisgender in the second. Both cases tie gender identity to a broader social identity, which in the case of the hijra is overtly religious. Many religions have produced bodily mutilation-improvement practices. In a chapter in *Sexual Muti-lations: A Human Tragedy*, Didier Diers and Xavier Valla discuss such practices, including male and female circumcisions, in the Abrahamic religions Judaism, Christianity, and Islam.[67] One especially dramatic example is the Skoptzy, a radical Christian group that emerged in eighteenth-century Russia and apparently still exists today.[68] Male members of the group had themselves castrated, and female members had their breasts amputated and vulvas removed, to demonstrate their rejection of carnal desires and, more significantly, to revert to a paradisaical asexual state prior to original sin. Here the improvement hoped to be achieved by the mutilation was soteriological: spiritual and religious salvation. While directly related to their sexuality, the sincere commitment of the Skoptzy practitioners goes beyond their gender roles and ultimately aims at their religious identity as extraordinarily devoted Christians.

Bodily mutilation-improvement of one's identity is not limited to regimes of sincerity; it can also occur in any other identity technology. A most radical postreligious case, if only a fictional one, occurs within the framework of authenticity. This is the suicide of Alexei Nilych Kirillov in Fyodor Dostoevsky's novel *Demons* (1871–72). Kirilov belongs to a group of nihilist revolutionary anarchists around whom the plot of the novel revolves. He is an atheist who believes in the radical autonomy and authenticity of the individual rather than in God. He must prove that he is a truly self-determined individual by overcoming all fear of death and autonomously deciding when to die. In this way even his death is authentically created rather than arbitrarily imposed by external powers. Consequently, Kirillov kills himself. His suicide is an extreme body mutilation-improvement under a self-imposed regime of authenticity. By taking his own life, Kirillov perfects his personal originality.

Since "true" authenticity tends to regard gender identity as secondary or non-authentic, it is difficult to find examples of gender-related bodily mutilation-improvement under regimes of authenticity. In profilicity, however, gender becomes once more a core identity marker. A relatively benign example of profilic gender-focused mutilation-improvement is male bodybuilding with the help of anabolic steroids. People knowingly use somewhat medically risky substances to boost their gender profile by

achieving a more "manly" appearance. This is roughly compa-
rable to female plastic surgery whereby women may have, for
instance, their breasts reshaped, in the hope of improving their
profiles in gender-related social-validation feedback loops.

In *The Myth of the Wrong Body*, Miquel Missé reflects on the
gender-affirmative medical procedures he went through. They
can also be understood as bodily mutilation-improvements aimed
at identity enhancement. Clearly, these procedures differ, for
example, from traditional Chinese footbinding or hijra castration through their not being aimed at embellishing gender-role
conformity. They do not occur within a regime of sincerity.
Moreover, the purpose of those procedures is to make people
look more *like* the gender they identify with. This distinguishes
them, notwithstanding the authenticity vocabulary that is used
to market them, from a radically authentic pursuit of uniqueness and originality. Gender-affirming surgery is based on the
idea that modifying one's body is needed to acquire and express
a person's best possible selfhood under conditions of profilicity.
While normally there are no traditional religious identifications
involved in gender-affirming surgery, it can arguably have a civil-
religious dimension and manifest a person's true investment in
being "progressive."

MAOISM

Since it became fashionable in the twelfth century, footbinding
always had its critics; it was not universally welcome in China
and, especially not by non-Han Chinese people. For example,
the rulers of the last Chinese imperial dynasty, the Qing (1644–
1911), who were ethnic Manchu, "forbade Manchu girls to bind
their feet and throughout their rule gave numerous orders to stop

the practice among Han women."[69] These orders, however, hardly diminished the popularity of the practice. It began to recede only with China's transition to modernity, which, in turn, was influenced by the Western colonialist impact that became particularly strong in the nineteenth century. During this time, the perception of footbinding changed drastically. Traditionally it had been seen as a symbol of refinement and cultivation, but in the face of modernity it increasingly appeared, to the contrary, as a symbol of Chinese backwardness and cultural deficiency—it was seen as "barbaric" and a sign of being "uncivilized." Wang Ping writes:

> Toward the end of the nineteenth century and at the beginning of the twentieth century, however, Chinese intellectuals, led by Kang Youwei and Liang Qichao, launched an antifootbinding propaganda campaign as part of the larger movement for reform, modernization, and feminine equality in China. Their main arguments were that footbinding made China an object of ridicule in the world, prevented the nation from taking its rightful place in international affairs, and weakened the country to a perilous degree by producing weak offspring.[70]

That modernist Chinese intellectuals felt that footbinding looked bad in the eyes of (Western) others was in part due to the fact that Anglo-American Protestant missionaries had publicly opposed it.[71] The forces of modernization were also the forces of the "age of authenticity," which perceived footbinding as a symbol of an old and vanishing regime of sincerity that tied women all too brutally to their gender roles and prevented them from becoming modern individuals.

Modernization and Westernization in China also gave rise to the founding of the Communist Party of China (CPC) in

Shanghai in 1921. Since its inception, the CPC vehemently opposed footbinding and saw itself, true to its Marxist roots, as the most radical political force for the liberation of women. Under the leadership of Mao Zedong (Mao Tse Tung), the CPC eventually came to power in 1949, and it remains in power today. Mao himself emphasized the interdependence between gender equality and the communist restructuring of society. In the Little Red Book he is quoted as saying, "Genuine equality between the sexes can only be realized in the process of the socialist transformation of society as a whole."[72] According to the Maoist (or Chinese Marxist) view, gender relations were an effect of the sociopolitical structures and the "mode of production" of a given era—in the case of premodern China, this view held, the Confucian tradition had produced a repressive gender ideology reflecting the feudal order. A standard exposition of this view is found in "Doctrine of Confucius and Mencius— The Shackle That Keeps Women in Bondage," by Fu Wen, published in the *Peking Review* in 1974:

> The Confucian ethics including the concept of "male superiority and female inferiority," played an extremely reactionary role in the course of the change from the slave system to the feudal system in Chinese society. But when the former had been completely destroyed and the latter firmly established, the landlord class inherited the whole lot of Confucian ethics out of its need to consolidate feudal autocratic rule. So feudal society remained a society with a patriarchal hierarchy. Promoted with might and main by the successive feudal dynasties and energetically trumpeted by the followers of Confucius, the reactionary Confucian viewpoint advocating the oppression of women became more concrete and more systematized than ever.[73]

Fu Wen then lists the traditional Confucian "three obediences and four virtues" of women as a paradigmatic expression of the Confucian gender hierarchy.[74]

> A female was placed under the control of the male sex from the cradle to the grave. The "four virtues" are firstly "women's virtue," meaning a woman must know her place under the sun and behave herself and act in every way in compliance with the old ethical code; secondly, "women's speech," meaning a woman must not talk too much and take care not to bore people; thirdly, "women's appearance," meaning a woman must pay attention to adorning herself with a view to pleasing the opposite sex; and fourthly, "women's chore," meaning a woman must willingly do all the household chores.[75]

It is plain to see that the "three obediences" and "four virtues" outline a strict gender hierarchy based on the assignment of gender roles—which indeed by and large framed the lives of women under traditional Chinese patriarchy and provided the rationale for gender practices such as female footbinding. One of the main goals of the Maoist revolution in China was to end the Confucian gender role regime once and for all. But what was supposed to replace it?

A communist country ought to be led by the productive forces, the workers and farmers, which, in turn, ought to be gender-equal. According to communist socioeconomic logic, the emancipation of women, based on equal pay and political power, would fully integrate them into the labor force, which would thereby be considerably strengthened. "It has become necessary to arouse the great mass of women who did not work in the fields before to take their place on the labor front," Mao is quoted as saying in the Little Red Book. "China's women are a vast reserve of labor power. This reserve should be tapped in the struggle to build a great socialist country."[76] Soong Ching Ling, a major female leader in Maoist China, outlined this idea in some detail in "Women's Liberation in China," published in the *Peking Review* in 1972. She wrote that prior to the revolution, "numerous women threw themselves into all kinds of revolutionary work" and "were eagerly devoted to their various tasks, with self-sacrificing spirit to fulfil the orders given by the Party." Once the revolution had succeeded, Soong Ching Ling wrote,

more and more women enlisted themselves in the army, navy, and air forces. They voluntarily entered these services after having passed a physical examination. More and more women joined agricultural field work, pasturage, mining, foundry, irrigation, communication, transportation, all kinds of factories, commerce, shop work, and various other public services. Since 1966, the first year of our Cultural Revolution, which is a part of the socialist revolution, the number of women doctors and nurses has been greatly increased. In very recent years, in a few large cities, all healthy women under forty-five have been given work in manufacture, commerce, communication, transportation, and other services for the people. Middle school graduates, boys as well as girls, have been allocated to work in factories, fields, and shops. Whatever men can do in these services women can equally do. By and large every woman who can work can take her place on the labor front, under the principle of equal pay for equal work. A large majority of the Chinese women have now attained their economic independence.[77]

Soong concluded that "genuine equality between the sexes can be realized . . . when and only when, led by a Marxist-Leninist political party, the process of the social transformation of society as a whole is completed . . . and when the feudal-patriarchal and other exploiting-class ideologies are completely uprooted."[78]

From a Maoist perspective, the two core differences between gender relations in the old "feudal patriarchy" and the new communist society take the form of "unequal vs. equal" and "unproductive vs. productive." The complete equalization of gender roles is supposed to bring about a radical change for women: no longer excluded from the main socioeconomic and political forces, they will join men on equal footing. This inclusion, it is implied, will abolish gender roles, or at least make them almost irrelevant. Female gender roles are supposed to be replaced by gender-neutral roles in agriculture and industry in the Marxist-Leninist political party and in the army. Following the examples of the female revolutionary avant-garde who had "devoted" themselves to their tasks in order "to fulfil the orders given by the Party," communist women, as Soong said, "enlist themselves," "enter services," and are "given" or "allocated" work. In short, the communist revolution, it is stipulated, has replaced hierarchical, unfree, and unproductive gender roles with nonhierarchical, free, and productive socioeconomic roles. In the terminology of this book, this means that an old regime of sincerity has been replaced with a new one. The identity technology—sincere commitment to roles—has remained the same, but the roles have been altogether "degendered" and instead politicized. It should be added, though, that in Maoist China the complete degenderization of roles happened more in theory than in practice.[79]

TRUE INVESTMENT

Saying that a transgender person is "trapped in the wrong body" is meant to empower their agency and give them the means to align their body with their true self. The law, the state, society, and the medical system are supposed to serve authentic individuals in their pursuit of getting their genders right.

There are alternatives, however, to "being" one's gender and to building a gendered sense of self. Under regimes of sincerity, the strategy was to commit to gendered social roles. This strategy was not limited to people who neatly aligned with the male–female sex binary. Some societies developed third gender roles that expanded—but did not challenge—patriarchal role hierarchies. Some biological men, such as the hijra, were allowed, or supposed, to live as "neither men nor women," and some biological women, such as the burrneshat chose, to be, or were designated to live as, "female-men." In any case, the way of identifying with one's gender was to internalize and enact the way of life that had been stipulated by society. Sometimes men, women, or third genders were encouraged to demonstrate their gender commitments by submitting themselves to bodily mutilations that were regarded, by themselves and/or others, as improvements of their identities. Practices such as castration or footbinding could enhance the moral, social, or religious value of a person. They proved the sincerity of one's commitment to one's gender identity.

Under conditions of profilicity, true investment in one's gender identity can emerge out of positive social-validation feedback loops. One can show investment in one's profile by making it cute or pretty. Fa, the transwoman from Taiwan, makes sure she looks after her hair and nails so as to get positive feedback on her femininity. In her stand-up comedy act, Irene Tu makes fun of her choice to brand herself as a cool, skateboarding lesbian rather than as a really boring nonbinary person. True investment in a gender profile can also be achieved by submitting oneself to gender-affirming medical procedures. Similar to regimes of sincerity, such practices in profilicity may enhance the social status and perceived validity of a person's gender identity.

The pursuit of originality, the commitment to a role, or the true investment in a profile are all viable technologies to achieve a strong sense of gendered self. How well these technologies work depends on the social conditions in which they are practiced. None is better or worse as such, and none is truer to what or who people "really are."

4

TRANSGENDER AND THE AUTHENTICITY NARRATIVE

TRANSGENDER AND THE ZEITGEIST

Not that long ago, in the latter part of the last century, transgender was at the fringes of society. It was a curiosity, depicted either in a starkly negative way—as in the cruel twistedness of a dangerous psychopath in *The Silence of the Lambs*, the still-famous 1991 movie—or, in a positive way, as a quirky but hip counterculture, provocatively and comically challenging a boring mainstream sexuality and a conformist moralism. For the latter, think of Lou Reed's iconic song "Walk on the Wild Side" (1972) or the Kinks' pop hit "Lola" (1970).

Times have changed. Today transgender is at the heart of the cultural and political wars raging not only, but most forcefully, in North America and Europe. It even plays a symbolic role in the physical war in Ukraine. To signal its difference from a supposedly decadent West indulging in sexual "perversions," Russia made a point of publicly rejecting and legally restricting anything to do with LGBTQ+, while, at least briefly, Ukraine made a point of visibly embracing LGBTQ+ and the liberal values associated with it by employing the American trans woman and political activist Sarah Ashton-Cirillo as an official military spokesperson.

But transgender did more than just hit a cultural nerve. Not only has it become a politically divisive issue and a ubiquitous media topic embedded in everything from the Oscars to TV commercials, in recent years transgender has also taken an arguably unprecedented existential hold on young people in many parts of the world. It is reported in a wide range of media sources that numbers of transgender people have grown exponentially. The *New York Times* spoke of a "stark generational shift in the growth of the transgender population of the United States."[1] A meta-analysis of data from twenty-three countries (all but one of them Western) between 1958 and 2014 estimates that transgender people accounted for 0.0046 percent of the general population during this period.[2] But then, according to a 2021 study on U.S. high schools, 9.2 percent of students reported a gender-diverse identity.[3] Studies conducted in a range of countries document an especially sharp rise in teenagers who are biologically born as girls and identify as boys.[4] Data from the Amsterdam Cohort of Gender Dysphoria Study in the Netherlands show that of the transgender youth (aged 13–16.9 years) who received puberty-suppression treatment, 69 percent were assigned female at birth, in contrast to 31 percent assigned male at birth.[5] If you live in a Western country today, chances are much increased, in comparison with the twentieth century, that transgender plays a role in your life or in the life of someone you know.

Why did this happen? Why did transgender, within the very short span of just a few years, rise from social obscurity to the center of attention? The answer suggested here is that this rapid shift, in terms both of (1) the number of people in whose life gender identity is a, if not *the*, crucial focal point, and (2) the concern with gender identity everywhere in society—in politics,

media, the law, academia, education, medicine, and so on—
reflects an ongoing long-term shift of the zeitgeist. Here, zeitgeist is meant not in the literal sense of a specific spiritual state
defining a historical era but refers to a shift in the dominant *identity technology*. The argument is that we are currently moving
from an "age of authenticity" into an "age of profilicity." This is
to say that people's sense of who they are is no longer built mainly
through the pursuit of originality but instead through the curation of profiles, including gender profiles.

Sexuality and gender can be core aspects of personal identity.
Naturally, a shift in the making of identity influences the making of gender. The current instability of gender categories—that
is, the reorientation in gender issues throughout society—is a
symptom of the breakdown of an old and the emergence of a new
identity technology. If we want to understand the extraordinary
social and political fascination with gender today and, in particular, the tumultuous changes in gender formation among ever
larger numbers of adolescents, we need to gain a better understanding of the demise of authenticity. We must understand its
instability due to inner contradictions, and, crucially, we must
understand the rise of profilicity: the shaping of a sense of self
and of one's gender in orientation to a profile.

Transgender has been many different things. For some individuals their biological sex, psychological sense of gender, and
socially ascribed and enacted gender do not match. A person may
have a masculine body but feel feminine and therefore uncom-
fortable if socially coerced to behave as a man and to meet social
expectations of men. In the language of twentieth-century Western medicine and up until 2013, this was called "gender identity
disorder." That term has been replaced by "gender dysphoria,"
but this designation too has been challenged because it continues to indicate a pathology. The notion of gender identity

disorder corresponded to a conception of *trans*gender that emphasized, because of an unbearable psychological incongruity regarding sex and gender, the eventual *transitioning* of a person from one gender to another. These transgender people were considered to have acquired at some point in their lives, for reasons largely unknown, a psychological disorder that made them desire to live as a person of a different gender.

Different forms of transgender are the so-called third genders discussed in the preceding chapter. One example mentioned there is the group known by the Urdu-language term "khawaja sira." This is a marginalized and impoverished group of biological males discriminated against in Pakistan. They dress and behave in feminine ways, similar to those of the hijras in India, but in an Islamic rather than a Hindu context. As Mobeen Azhar explains in an article in *The World*, most khawaja siras are "making a living from performance, sex work, or begging. They are simultaneously celebrated as 'gifted' by God and ridiculed for not conforming to the male/female gender roles that society prescribes."[6] Importantly, they identify and are identified as "neither male nor female" and are believed "to be 'God's chosen people,' with special powers to bless and curse."[7] Their gender is religiously grounded as of divine origin and accordingly regarded as immutable and acquired since conception. It is not seen as a personal choice, and it is not possible to transition to or away from being a khawaja sira. Khawaja sira people tend to reject being called "transgender" if that implies being a woman who was assigned the male sex at birth. Mobeen Azhar quotes a khawaja sira person strongly dismissing that label: "These people who say they are transgender; that concept is just wrong. . . . They can never be women. They cannot give birth. Even if they change their bodies, they can't change who they are. We are not women. We are what Allah has made."[8] Khawaja siras behave and dress like khawaja siras. Their gender experience may not be dysphoric—they probably feel like khawaja siras, and others in their society will "properly" address and treat them as khawaja siras. They can be considered *trans*gender in the sense that their gender *transcends* the "normal" gender binary male–female.

The diversity of transgender as biological, psychological, or social incongruity or as a peculiar third gender, shows that transgender is shaped within specific social conditions. In nineteenth-century Pakistan, no one could be treated as "having gender identity disorder"—that medical classification did not exist. Similarly, for a person who grows up in the suburbs in the United States of today, it is basically impossible to live as a khawaja sira, since no such group exists in that society. Neither do its specific roles, restrictions, and expectations.

The khawaja sira is a transgender identity in a society that operates primarily with the identity technology of sincerity—the development of a sense of identity acquired by sincerely committing to socially prescribed roles, including gender roles. Like people whose gender identity is formed by committing to male or female roles, a khawaja sira can form a gendered sense of self by committing to the social roles of a khawaja sira, for better or worse.

The concept of gender identity disorder belongs to the age of authenticity, when gender roles were no longer regarded as definite or essential. The concept was applied to people who were treated as unfortunately afflicted by a rare psychological illness. To cure this peculiar illness, there were basically two options. (1) Fix their mind, through psychotherapy in the hope of aligning their psychological gender experience with their bodily sex. The therapeutic hope was that if people suffered from the desire to live as someone of a gender different form their biological sex, the suffering might then disappear if the desire disappeared.

This approach, however, came to be regarded as "conversion therapy" and is now no longer considered appropriate and is often outlawed. (2) Fix their body, by surgery or other medical procedures, so that it matched their psychological gender experience. The belief behind these procedures was that, owing to their presumed mental illness, artificial body modification suggesting a physical transition to the opposite sex was required for some people to be well. But this didn't really affect a person's authenticity, since authenticity was found in a nongendered unique individual self, no matter if one happened to be male, female, or transitioned from one to the other for psychological reasons.

To be clear, under the paradigm of authenticity, if an inauthentic person, a complete *Spießbürger*, a boring normie who just followed all the conventions and lacked any originality, happened to suffer from gender dysphoria, and, with medical assistance, switched from male to female to feel better, then this transition may not have made the person more authentic at all. They might remain the same *Spießbürger* they had always been. Conversely, if a superauthentic person, who had been completely true to themselves and always pursued originality, happened to develop a disturbing gender identity disorder and for this reason underwent a sex change, then the procedure might heal them psychologically and would do nothing to decrease their authenticity.

To sum up, under conditions of sincerity, when gender identity was formed in orientation to gender roles, transgender transcended the common dual gender roles of male and female to make a third gender role. Under conditions of authenticity, transgender emphasizes a transition from one gender to another but, since authenticity was not tied to gender, the transition per se did not diminish or increase a person's authenticity. One's authenticity and uniqueness did not hinge on living as male or female or on having transitioned from one to the other.

In our present age of profilicity, people shape their identities by curating profiles that they can be truly invested in. This true investment takes shape in social-validation feedback loops, exemplified most clearly on social media, but it is by no means restricted to these. Unlike in authenticity, but as in sincerity, gender in profilicity becomes once more a *defining* aspect of one's identity. In sincerity, roles were gendered, and in profilicity, profiles are often gendered as well. Different from sincerity, though, gender is no longer enacted in conformity to specific roles and, accordingly, transgender in profilicity is not a specific third gender with distinctive expectations and limitations.

*Trans*gender today can mean transitioning within and/or transcending the male–female duality, and this can be done in myriad ways. Wikipedia lists more than one hundred gender identities, most of which can be associated with the umbrella term "transgender."[9] Any of these new transgender identities can be part of a person's profile. Transgender under conditions of profilicity is not better or worse than but rather different from transgender under conditions of sincerity and authenticity, and these differences need to be better understood. Probably the main obstacle to understanding them is that profilic transgender still tends to be described in the language of authenticity. The deeply paradoxical claim to authenticity of transgender today must be questioned.

CONTRAPOINTS: "YOU WANT THEM TO SEE YOU LIKE THEY SEE EVERY OTHER GIRL"

ContraPoints is one of the most successful YouTube channels presenting philosophy content. A video on the *Twilight* saga, a popular series of vampire romance novels, was published only five days prior to writing this sentence.[10] The video—almost three hours long and nicely ending on a Daoist note—already has more than 1.8 million views. The host of the channel is Natalie Wynn, a transgender woman with an academic background in philosophy. Her videos are characterized by elaborate and subtle aesthetics. They are eloquently and intelligently scripted and very professionally performed. Many of the videos on the channel are about transgender.

In "Pronouns," one of the videos on transgender, Wynn expresses a critical awareness of the fuzziness of the notion of gender identity: "All this talk about gender identity, a lot of the time I don't really get it either."[11] She asks herself, "Am I really, truly a woman, ontologically, neurologically, metaphysically?" She then replies, "Well, honestly, I don't even know what that would mean."[12] There is no essence to gender identity, Wynn indicates. There is nothing substantially and eternally determined a priori as "masculine" or "feminine." In another video, in a critique of *Harry Potter* author J. K Rowling, who has been accused of being transphobic, Wynn calls the attempt to define "woman" in terms of gender a "bullshit semantic debate" and concludes, "This is metaphysics, and life is too short for metaphysics."[13] It is not just that gender metaphysics is a waste of time for Wynn; "I personally don't believe in any gender metaphysics at all," she declares.[14]

Wynn suggests that if there is no gender metaphysics, there is also no "gender theology."[15] Gender identity is not assigned to individuals by God, and the sex binary is not a divine creation. What is more, if gender identity has no supernatural origin, neither is it, in a secularized version of gender theology, something that a person is "meant to be" or "born with." "I wasn't born a woman," Wynn quips. "I was born a fucking baby."[16] In reality, gender identity is not imposed on people by a higher power; it is contingent on evolving circumstances. Consequently, Wynn opposes the "feminine-essence theory," which says that "trans women are female souls in male bodies" and "essentially women from birth to death" and who transition to make their "accidental exterior match [their] essential interior."[17] This rejection of a feminine-essence theory can be extended to any gender-essence theory. Clearly, for Wynn, gender identity is not an innate characteristic of a person's "soul," "brain," "mind," or "spirit"; it is not a quality of any "original self."

While denying any metaphysical or theological grounding of gender identity, Wynn accepts biological distinctions between the sexes. "No trans person thinks it's possible to change chromosomal sex," she says, adding that "when transphobes say sex is real, they are not actually contradicting anything most trans people believe."[18] For Wynn, as for Simone de Beauvoir, gender identity is a socially and psychologically constructed reality and thereby distinct from biological sex.

Wynn rejects not only the metaphysical or theological idea of a gendered essence that characterizes each self but also the authentic quest for a true self beyond gender. She satirically depicts the impossibly quixotic demand of some radical feminists to abolish gender altogether in order to achieve true equality between the sexes.[19] If you take away all the gendered aspects of a person, nothing of her remains. For Wynn, the purely authentic genderless true self is just as much a fiction as the gendered soul.

Wynn's post-authentic understanding of gender identity and especially of her own identity as a trans woman is developed out of a critical reflection on Judith Butler's conception of gender as performative.[20] For Wynn, gender is a "series of gestures." She elaborates: "It's the way you dress, it's the way you speak, it's the way you act, it's the way you relate to other people."[21] Her "post-Butlerian" understanding of gender identity is in effect *profilic*, although she does not use this term.

In her video "Pronouns," Wynn reiterates that gender identity cannot be reduced to inner psychology or to what people think or feel their gender is: "If psychological identity was the only thing that mattered, there would be no need for a trans person to come out or do anything to transition, including requesting different pronouns, because pronouns belong to the social world of language, not to individual psychology." Gender is not just an idea or a feeling; it is "also social, structural, and interpersonal." This is to say, being a woman, for example, depends on social validation, on being publicly treated *as a woman*. Wynn provides a pertinent example: "You know, you don't become a woman the first time you put on a dress; you become a woman the first time an older female relative turns to you at a restaurant and says, 'Maybe you should order the salad, sweetie.'"[22] As a trans woman, she wants to be treated and seen in terms of how women are treated and seen in society: "We want not necessarily to pass perfectly, but at least to seem like our genders to the people around us. As Laura Jane Grace put it, 'You want them to see you like they see every other girl.'" With this quote, Wynn perfectly illustrates gender under the conditions of profilicity— and its difference from the authentic pursuit of originality.

"All I can really tell you is that I prefer to express myself with diaphanous feminine gestures," Wynn says, describing her sense of gender identity, "that taking female hormones and having feminizing medical procedures makes me feel more at home in my body, and that I like it when other people treat me as a woman, socially, spiritually, sexually."[23] For her, what matters is not to take on traditional gender roles (such as that of a housewife) but to be *treated in a gendered way*, "socially, spiritually, sexually." She points out that, in the present world, such gender profile validation can be especially important on social media: "A lot of extremely online trans people really don't have a strong sense of conviction in their own identity, which is why they need constant external validation to prop them up. They need to be constantly told that they're valid, that they really are the gender they say they are."[24] It is probably fair to say that Wynn, with her millions of viewers, also qualifies in a way as an "extremely online trans person." In fact, most people today, including myself, are "extremely online." The "extreme" has become the new normal. In such an extremely online world, profilic gender identity thrives.

In profilicity, how the gendered body image is seen by others is of prime importance. Wynn confirms this: "I am not like, 'Ah, yeah, I have tits now, that's so hot. I mean it's kind of hot, but it's more about other people being into it than it is about me being into it.' "[25] She longs for the genuine validation of her feminine appearance and "diaphanous feminine gestures" because her emotional well-being depends on it: "I am afraid that people will never take me seriously, hence ruining any chance I have at happiness."[26] Referring to feminist Katherine McKinnon, Wynn emphasizes that gender identity lies in its successful presentation: "Anybody who identifies as a woman, wants to be a woman, is going around being a woman, as far as I am concerned, is a woman."[27] This is to say that gender identity hinges on the curation of a profile or, as Wynn says, on successfully "prompting others": "We're using a cultural language of feminine signifiers to prompt others to see us for what we are."[28] Her transition is, in her words, oriented toward "presenting in such a meticulously feminine way."[29] Or, as she says in her latest video, "gender expression is not just aesthetic, it's style."[30]

The self-reflective analysis of transgender identity on *ContraPoints* is a striking outline of gender—not just transgender, but any gender—under conditions of profilicity. Wynn's You-Tube videos subtly contradict current narratives about gender that spread the myth of the wrong body. Against all the evidence pointing to gender as profile, these narratives still tend to be stuck in the language of the age of authenticity. But why?

MCLUHAN'S REARVIEW MIRROR

"We look at the present through a rear-view mirror," the avant-garde media theorist Marshall McLuhan said in the 1960s. "We march backwards into the future."[31] This image was meant to illustrate the idea that when a society develops new technologies that change its very fabric, it still tends to rely on older cultural narratives and conceptual frameworks to make sense of a radically altered world. To reduce the potentially frightening unfamiliarity of new ways of life created by new media, we seek comfort in telling ourselves bygone stories. While moving into an enigmatic future, we explain the present in the reassuring terms of the past. McLuhan explained this phenomenon further with an example: "Suburbia lives imaginatively in *Bonanza* land."[32] *Bonanza* was an exceedingly popular TV show that ran in the United States from 1959 to 1973. It was set in the old "Wild West"—that is, on the nineteenth-century American frontier, where descendants of European immigrants lived a largely preindustrial life. The old-fashioned rural world of people on horseback that the show presented contrasted sharply with its viewers' postindustrial reality, shaped as it was by modern housing, TV sets, and cars. Put in the theoretical vocabulary of this book, while the millions of American viewers of *Bonanza* lived in the age of authenticity, they nostalgically looked at their country in the rearview mirror image where it appeared as *Bonanza* land. And this *Bonanza* land was a sincerity land.

Today's North American and European gender narratives function similarly. While society has already moved on to the age of profilicity, it envisions itself in the semantics and the ideology of the age of authenticity. This is particularly obvious in the language and the iconography that frames new forms of transgender. In today's rearview mirror, we see gender not in the guise of the simulated sincerity of a *Bonanza* land but in a land of simulated authenticity. While identity, including transgender identity, is in fact already shaped by the technology of profilicity, it is still often nostalgically depicted and celebrated in an image of authenticity.

BEING UNAPOLOGETICALLY YOURSELF

In her column "Ask Stacey" in *The Dundalk Eagle*, Stacey Hurley explains that the process of gender transition is a journey toward physically matching the "inner self" so that people can finally reach "their authentic selves." To illustrate her point, she quotes a transgender person named Sara J.: "One of life's great struggles lies in searching for authenticity. We seek authenticity in the jobs we choose and the jobs we flee, in the friends we make and those we keep, in the clothes we choose and the way we present ourselves to the world. . . . To me, authenticity—finding my authentic self—meant solving my lifelong puzzle: a mismatch between my inner self and my body."[33]

Inman, an online platform dedicated to the real estate industry, is ripe with advertising. It posted a short piece by Jamie Zapata, "a Realtor and LGBTQ+ advocate based in San

Antonio, Texas," for whom "leading with authenticity in both life and business is the only way to thrive."[34] Using the collective pronoun "we," she promotes the authenticity of all LGBTQ+ people: "We are unapologetically ourselves." But then it gets a little confusing. She writes: "Being trans is no more of a choice than it is for anyone else to be who they are. Non-LGBTQ+ people get to decide who they are, and how they want to present themselves to the world, so trans people should be afforded that same luxury." Maintaining that being transgender cannot be chosen, Zapata demands that transgender people ought to be empowered to decide their gender identity. But how can one decide to be what one cannot choose to be? The confusion is not really resolved in what follows: "Recognizing us for who we are and not our appearance or sexuality can help trans people feel more comfortable when working with us as clients." Here, Jamie Zapata demands that transgender people not be judged by their "appearance or sexuality." This sounds reasonable. But then again, isn't this "appearance or sexuality" precisely what transgender people show once they do what Jamie Zapata encouraged them to do, "present themselves to the world?"

Authenticity vibes reverberate throughout the depiction of transgender in mass and social media. The book *Authentic Selves: Celebrating Trans and Nonbinary People* (2023) is advertised on Amazon as "a sweeping compilation of life stories and portraits of trans and nonbinary people, as well as their partners, parents, children, siblings, and chosen family members."[35] In both text and photography, it promises to combine touching tales of pursuing individual authenticity with "stunning photographs," as the description on Amazon highlights, and stories about the achievements of exemplary transgender persons such as "Senator Sarah McBride, disability justice advocate Parker Glick, drag entertainer TAYLOR ALXNDR, September 11th first responder

Jozeppi Angelo Morelli, model Lana Patel, youth activist Elliott Bertrand, and so many others." In *Authentic Selves*, the pursuit of an authenticity narrative is woven into the fabric of the pursuit of the American Dream, and it highlights visibility in media, entertainment, and politics. In transgender, too, it is suggested, the celebration of authenticity can pave the way to celebrity status. The authenticity language of the book's marketing extends to the finer details: Coauthor Jeanette Jennings, the Amazon description informs potential buyers, "is married to her *soulmate* Greg" (emphasis added).

Amazon not only sells books about finding authenticity in transgender. On Amazon Prime Video, it also offers a TV series on the subject. *Always Jane* "follows two years in the life of Jane Noury, a transgender teenager living in rural New Jersey."[36] The ingredients of *Always Jane* are very similar to those of *Authentic Selves*: a combination of (1) a story of authenticity pursuit and discovery of one's true self, (2) the American Dream story of making a white-collar career in, and perhaps even beyond, the American middle class, and (3) a focus on becoming a celebrity and on the presentation of glamorous images. The TV series shows Jane "fly across the country to participate in trans modeling agency Slay's first modeling competition."[37] As the series title indicates, Jane has "always" been Jane, and not Jack, her assigned male name at birth. *Always Jane* is advertised as a coming-of-age story, a TV version of a traditional Bildungsroman. The coming of age consists in the protagonist finding and becoming her correctly gendered self while undergoing surgery. The series is touted as a dramatic revelation of how Jane and her family "tackle obstacles head-on so that Jane can live authentically."[38] This struggle toward authenticity, however, is at the same time also a competitive effort to become a successful model in the media and fashion industry.

Always Jane received mixed reviews. *The Guardian* praised it as "a striking new Amazon Prime series." The reviewer Adrian Horton noted that it is "marked by the classic emotional roller-coaster of friendships, family and figuring out who you are" and therefore is, in essence, about becoming one's authentic self.[39] Largely ignoring the modeling business story line, Horton is especially enthralled by the series' politically and morally progressive take on transgender. Kristen Lopez in her review in *Indiewire* also focuses on the series' main theme of the pursuit of authenticity and calls it an "exploration of finding oneself," albeit a "far too simple" one.[40] She points to some features of Jane's depiction that don't necessarily support the authenticity narrative of the series—for instance, most of Jane's "friendships are conducted on Instagram" and she has a "penchant for throwing duck lips." What is more, Lopez finds the celebration of Jane's quest to be herself ultimately rather too corny. "The problem is the entire affair, too often, feels like inspiration porn," Lopez writes. "Where the joy for the audience is going to be seeing how inspiring Jane is—and little else." What Lopez depicts as "inspiration porn" could, arguably more aptly, also be called authenticity porn.

MEDICINE AS IDENTITY TECHNOLOGY

The two main story lines of *Always Jane* are her modeling career and her medical transition. In episode 4, when still in the hospital, recovering from her surgery, Jane sees her new vagina in the mirror for the first time. Turning to her mother she says, cheerily, "That looks like a vagina, right?" Her mother laughingly confirms. Later on, Jane shows her vagina to her friend and asks seriously, "What would you say my vagina looks like?" The friend replies, "Any other vagina." Jane is very happy with this response. The acquisition of a vagina that looks like "any other" is a highlight in her successful journey toward authenticity.

In America (but not only there, of course), the surgical production of vaginas that look like any other has become a fastgrowing and increasingly profitable business. CNN reports that "gender-affirming surgeries done in the United States nearly tripled between 2016 and 2019."[41] According to Grand View Research, "the U.S. sex reassignment surgery market size was estimated at USD 2.1 billion in 2022 and is anticipated to grow at a compound annual growth rate (CAGR) of 11.25% from 2023 to 2030."[42] Where there is business, there is advertising, and where there is advertising, there is stereotypical storytelling. Advertising in the gender-affirming industry, not unlike advertising in the fashion industry, relies on the narrative of authenticity to sell a product that, it is suggested, will make purchasers feel more individual by looking more alike.

Here's how the company ART Surgical in San Francisco markets itself: "Welcome to ART Surgical founded by Dr. Angela Rodriguez. Our care center specializes in procedures for transgender and gender-diverse individuals. Your path to your true identity begins here." The text continues: "Every individual's journey is unique and deserves celebration. Our patient stories inspire us and show that self-discovery can lead to positive change. It takes courage, and we support your authenticity."[43] While pointing out that the "path to true identity" is unique for "every individual," ART Surgical promises that the effect of the procedures it offers is not to make people look more original or more different from one another but rather more similar. Those who decide for "masculinization surgery" will be made to look more like average men by "enhancing masculine features and proportions," and those who opt for "body feminization . . . designed to enhance feminine characteristics and proportions" will look more like typical women are expected to look like.

Gender and Sexual Health Services at Brown University caters to "youth who are transgender, gender diverse, or otherwise exploring their gender and sexual identity." Its explicit goal is to "help you be authentic and true to yourself in a safe and healthy way."[44] It explains that "gender and sexuality can be a part of every person's growing self identity; people identify with and express gender in a wide variety of ways, and gender and sexuality may be fluid and change over a person's lifetime."

The Hippocratic oath goes back to ancient Greece (ca. fifth to third century BCE). Since then, numerous variations of it have been at the center of mainstream Western medical ethics. The most common moral imperative associated with it is the negative decree "Do no harm." The health services advertised by Gender and Sexual Health Services at Brown go beyond such a minimalistic aspiration. They are guided by a more ambitious and proactive ethical imperative. Here, the main concern is not simply procedural caution but affirmation of the patient's "self identity." Going beyond traditional medical approaches focusing on a person's body and, by extension, their mental well-being, Brown's gender and sexual health unit digs deeper and wants to help people become their true self through medical procedures. According to its rationale, a person's health hinges on their being authentic, which in turn hinges on getting their gender identity right, which in turn can be aided by medical interventions. Medical services are advertised as support procedures in a person's identity work—which puts medical technology in the service of identity technology. It is *identity medicine*.

RESTROOM POLITICS

The marketing language of ART Surgical and of Gender and Sexual Health Services at Brown University employ the same trope of authenticity that appeals to the true self as the highest good. When it comes to transgender, medical procedures are advertised with the pathos of authenticity. Politics tends to do this as well. New York City was among of the first jurisdictions in the United States to grant and promote "bathroom rights" to transgender people, enabling them to use public restrooms that aligned with their declared gender identity. An advertising campaign launched by then-mayor Bill de Blasio in 2016 featured the slogan "Use the restroom consistent with who you are."[45] Formulated as a moral imperative, the slogan expresses the demand that bathroom usage ought to entail confirmation of a person's authenticity. Moreover, given that his name was on the public advertisements, the mayor was profiled by means of the political promise to empower people to be who they are.

Somewhat ironically, however, the political insistence on proving one's authenticity in the restroom has already become outdated. less than a decade old at the time of writing, de Blasio's slogan contradicts the more recent political trend to provide unisex public facilities—a measure that probably helps to avoid conflict. In a unisex restroom, people can relieve themselves without the necessity to simultaneously demonstrate consistency with who they truly are. Restroom use thereby becomes increasingly detached from the demonstration of identity.

While unisex restrooms can indeed provide a somewhat unexpected safe space for those who prefer not to be reminded of their gender identity in *everything* they do, the idea that displaying one's gender correctly is important to being truly oneself continues to reign supreme in gender politics. The LGBTQ+

organization Human Rights Campaign posted an online report titled "Coming Out: Living Authentically as Transgender or Non-Binary." Its most basic claim is that society, via politics, legislation, and culture, should enable transgender people to "live a happy life as your authentic self rather than trying to adapt to others' expectations of who you should be."[46] The authors of the report apparently did not realize the slight paradox that by encouraging transgender people to live "authentically *as* transgender," they also formulate a certain "expectation of who you should be."

THE AUTONOMOUS INDIVIDUAL

The idea—or ideal—that the true self is gendered appears throughout the academic literature on transgender as well. Academia has not avoided being heavily impacted by the current cultural and political wars waged over the issue. While there is, as far as I can see, scientific consensus on the significant increase of transgender prevalence in Western societies in the present century, the reasons for this increase are vigorously debated. The increase coincides suspiciously with the spread of social media. There is evidence, albeit disputed,[47] that some teenagers are triggered to identify as transgender by their social media activities and contacts or by mass media coverage of the topic.[48] The seemingly commonsense hypothesis that increased media presence and positive depiction of transgender has caused a higher transgender prevalence, especially among teenagers, has generated strong rebuttals, such as this one by the Human Rights Campaign: "You may see opponents of trans people specifically use junk science by Lisa Littman at Brown University to falsely claim that access to social media and the internet has created a 'contagion' that causes many youths to mistakenly identify as transgender."[49] The social-contagion hypothesis seems to have hit a nerve, as it contradicts the authenticity narrative. If, indeed, young transgender people decide who they are because of their media activities, they may have made their decision because of the influence of others.

Opponents of the social-contagion hypothesis will argue that the increase of transgender among young people is by no means *caused* by media but reflects a more tolerant society that, via its media, empowers more individuals to come out. As reported in the *New York Times*, "social media has been a significant catalyst for teenagers questioning their gender identities today."[50] The reporter suggests here that media like itself, by removing the stigma of transgender, make it easier for transgender people to self-identify their gender correctly. From this perspective, the media help individuals, and society in general, to become more authentic. If affirming one's transgender identity is all about being more authentic, the social-contagion hypothesis is not simply wrong; it is immoral, as implied in "Respecting the free will, authenticity and autonomy of transgender youth," published in the journal *Nursing Ethics*.[51] According to her LinkedIn page, author Leonie Cross is "passionate about ethics."[52] She writes that "it has been suggested in some studies that transness in young people is a result of peer contagion." For Cross, this suggestion is morally wrong because it could prevent those adolescents from "living a life true to a self-determined gender." She argues that "any discussion regarding peer or social contagion can potentially dissuade a healthcare professional, including nurses, from respecting free will, authenticity and autonomy of any TGD person, but especially TGD youth." Cross ends her paper with a passionate ethical plea to all nurses: "Nurses should lead the way in supporting TGD young people's free will, authenticity and autonomy, advocating for and empowering these unique and frequently vulnerable members of our community." For her, as for ART Surgical and Bill de Blasio, transgender is the front line where authenticity must be defended.

From a scientific perspective, the existence of authentic and autonomous selves remains questionable—there is little evidence to support the assumption that most of our actions, and much less our gender or our sex, can be ultimately traced back to "free will" as its root cause.[53] Instead, as outlined earlier, scientific research suggests that humans are conditioned in highly complex ways by our biology, our psychology, and social and historical factors, none of which we may control. And yet academic literature on transgender sometimes considers it controversial and morally inappropriate to assert that social influence is a factor in determining what we take to be our true selves and so to question the self-determination of gender identity. But isn't the very notion of a true self, with its free will and authenticity, already an idea supplied to many of us, including to Leonie Cross, by "social contagion" in our specific culture and times?

SELF-DETERMINATION OF GENDER IN THE LAW

Given how emphatically gender is connected with the key authenticity concepts of free will and autonomy, it is perhaps unsurprising that this relation has made its way through the media, politics, academia, and the medical industry into the law. On June 19, 2024, the German parliament approved a new law on the "self-determination" (*Selbstbestimmung*) of gender, which, similar to recently established laws in several other countries, is meant to enable individuals to decide by themselves, independently of their biological sex or the opinions of psychologists or other specialists, what their gender identity is.[54] The choice is then registered by the state in the form of a "gender entry" (*Geschlechtseintrag*). Notably, the German word *Geschlecht* can refer to both sex and gender—which can lead to considerable misunderstandings. Since the bill for this law explicitly equates the German word *Geschlechtsidentität* with "gender identity" in English-language documents,[55] however, it must be assumed that *Geschlecht* is understood as gender.

The carefully wrought bill was publicly debated by the German parliament in November 2023.[56] It is quite a stunning illustration of the numerous paradoxes and contradictions between an emerging profilic practice of (trans-)gender and its continued conceptualization in terms of authenticity.

A new law has become necessary, the bill states at the outset, because in recent years "the medical and social understanding of gender identity has further evolved."[57] While this is certainly the case, the bill doesn't clearly address *how* exactly this understanding has developed. This lack of clarity is telling, because an exact or commonly agreed-on medical or social definition of "gender identity" hardly exists. Is the gender identity that the law is concerned with biologically determined? And, if so, how exactly? Is it stable? Is it psychologically determined? Is it a feeling? Is it socially constructed? Or a mix of all those factors? And if so, what kind of mix?

The core contradiction of the bill is tied to the ambiguity of the German word *bestimmen*, which, like its English counterpart "determine," has two different meanings. To determine can mean either to find out what something objectively is (e.g., "The team determined the chemical composition of the mineral") or to make a subjective decision ("I am yet to determine how I will spend my sabbatical"). Replicating this ambiguity, the German bill at times seems to conceive of gender identity as something that is a definite and essential quality of a person, akin to the popular but unscientific notion of a gendered soul. In this sense the document speaks of gender identity as something that is "found" and "recognized" (*das Finden und Erkennen der eigenen geschlechtlichen Identität*).[58] This expression reflects the idea that authenticity hinges on finding and recognizing one's true self.

Mostly, however, the bill describes gender identity as a "gender feeling" or "gender sense." The German term for this is *Geschlechtsempfinden*.[59] *Empfinden* is a tricky word, too. It is derived from *finden* (to find), but unlike *finden* and *erkennen* (to find and to recognize) which imply rational understanding, *empfinden* is emotional; it is a "sensing" or "feeling." Moreover, like "to sense" in English, *empfinden* can relate to something that exists prior to and independent of the sensing. For instance, one can sense, or *empfinden*, cold temperature. But, on the other hand, *empfinden* can indicate a subjective emotion: One can *Liebe empfinden*—feel love. Unlike cold temperature, love *is* an *Empfindung*, a "feeling" or "sentiment." The legal document never clarifies how to conceive of *Geschlechtsempfinden*, or "gender feeling." Is it the sensing of what one objectively *is*, independent of the act of feeling (akin to temperature)? Or is gender identity a sentiment—an emotional or psychological state? And if it is a sentiment, is the sentiment something that overcomes me, that is contingent and beyond my control (akin to passionate love or hate)? Or is it an emotional expression of my deepest personal core, the articulation of my true self? Empirically, *Geschlechtsempfinden* is probably a contingent sentiment beyond our control. But, as we will see, legally it tends to be regarded as the sovereign expression of our true selfhood.

By *not* resolving the ambiguities of the term *Geschlechtsempfinden*, the legal document achieves a crucial rhetorical effect: It embeds the notion of gender identity even deeper in the language of authenticity. The philosopher Charles Taylor defined authenticity as involving three key components. The first of these is "(i) creation and construction as well as discovery."[60]

The true self at the heart of authenticity is supposed to be both constructed and discovered. Logically and empirically, this is contradictory. The philosophy of authenticity didn't reject this contradiction but embraced it as something valuable. From a philosophical perspective, this very contradiction can illustrate the complexity of authenticity. In Hegel's philosophical language, human selfhood is *an-und-für-sich*, or "in-and-for-itself." It is not merely objective and substantial (*an sich*, in itself), but also subjective and creative (*für sich*, for itself). The ambiguous notion of *Geschlechtsempfinden* suggests the same dialectical movement from objectivity to subjectivity, and thereby imbues the notion of gender identity with the same magic as the authentic self: Gender identity morphs from objective to subjective "being," from something one individual passively inherits to something exemplifying individual agency.

The German bill skillfully exploits the dialectical ambiguities of *Geschlechtsempfinden* (gender feeling) and *Selbstbestimmung* (self-determination) to give its notion of gender identity the aura of an equally ambiguous authenticity. Gender identity is not just discovered but created by the self. This movement from objective to subjective gender identity enables the individual to "own" their gender identity. In this way the legal document achieves a key goal: to connect gender identity with autonomy—a core value of the age of authenticity. Once gender identity has been transformed from a passively acquired characteristic into a self-produced sentiment, it makes sense to claim that it *must* be up to the individual, and *only* to the individual, to self-determine the gender identity to be registered by the state. Gender identity is now a matter of and for, and to be dealt with by, the true self—the law can enter the scene as the righteous protector of the individual's sovereignty over their gender. Almost triumphantly, the legal document takes the moral high ground and affirms that "human dignity in connection with the fundamental right to protection of the person makes it mandatory to take into account the right to self-determination of the concerned individual and to legally recognize their self-felt gender identity."[61] Accordingly, it mandates the "autonomous decision on the choice of gender" (*autonome Entscheidung über die Wahl des Geschlechts*).[62]

The essence of the seventy-five-page German bill can be succinctly summarized in the two sentences by Jamie Zapata quoted earlier: "Being trans is no more of a choice than it is for anyone else to be who they are. Non-LGBTQ+ people get to decide who they are, and how they want to present themselves to the world, so trans people should be afforded that same luxury." Starting from the assumption that gender identity is *not a choice*, the semantics and ideology of the age of authenticity transform gender identity dialectically into a matter that each individual *must decide autonomously*.

But importantly, Jamie Zapata's statement also perfectly summarizes how the German bill, despite all its elaborate authenticity dialectics, is ultimately not about authenticity but about profilicity, or about the right of individuals "to present themselves to the world." The law makes use of the rhetoric and complex ambiguities of authenticity to eventually prescribe and protect something altogether different, gender identity as presented, seen, and validated in public. While unable to present an empirically coherent conception of subjective gender identity based on *Geschlechtsempfinden*, the law is quite precise in its conception of the social gender identity that is publicly registered. This external gender identity is in reality what individuals, empowered by the new law, are supposed to self-determine. In effect, the gender identity at stake is the gender profile.

Charles Taylor's definition of authenticity adds two more key components to the mix of self-discovery and self-creation: "(ii) originality, and frequently (iii) opposition to the rules of society and even potentially to what we recognize as morality."[63] These two key components of authenticity, however, are conspicuously missing in the German law's approach to gender identity. Instead of emphasizing individual originality, the law emphasizes alignment of people with a transindividual gender. And instead of opposition to social and moral conventions, the law highlights coherence with them.

The stated purpose of the law is to allow transgender people to self-determine their officially registered gender identity so that they are enabled to "live [*leben*] in accordance with [*entsprechend*] their sensed gender [*Geschlecht*]."[64] Here the law assumes that lifestyles are gendered and that, to fully align with a lifestyle, it is necessary to officially register oneself as *being* a specific gender. This point is made quite explicit: "The assignment to [*Zuordnung zu*] a gender is of outstanding importance for individual identity under the given conditions. . . . Typically, [gender assignment] plays a key role in a person's sense of self as well as in how this person is perceived by others. . . . The gender to which a person belongs . . . determines, for instance, how a person is addressed, and what expectations are in place regarding their outward appearance, the education, and behavior of a person."[65]

The bill curiously departs from its earlier insistence on authenticity and autonomy and now claims that it is essential for everyone, but specifically transgender people, to be publicly assigned (*zugeordnet*) to a certain gender category. What is more, this gender assignment, the bill stipulates, "determines" (!) (*bestimmt*) how people are supposed to look and most of what they do. On the one hand it is stipulated that people must self-determine their gender assignment, but on the other it is presumed that one's gender category *determines* how one ought to live. Paradoxically, the text eventually formulates a law of self-determining how one is determined by one's gender. It "empowers" people to authentically decide in which way they will be non-authentic.

The bill's conception of gender as determining how people are expected to look and behave may seem awkwardly similar to the older regime of sincerity, the identity technology that shapes a person's sense of self in orientation to socially prescribed roles and especially to gender roles. From the above quote passages, it looks at first sight as if the German law desires transgender people to live like the khawaja sira in Pakistan: they ought to officially assign themselves to a gender that then obliges them to live in accordance with the social and moral norms imposed by their new gender role. If so, this would be a complete reversal of authenticity to the identity technology that it rejects.

But to be fair, this cannot be the spirit of the law—and it isn't. The law clearly presupposes modern gender equality and does not wish, for instance, to prescribe to male-to-female transgender individuals that they must live as housewives and not wear trousers. Moreover, it not only accepts the two traditional gender categories male and female but also allows one to choose among "diverse" categories or "none," thereby significantly widening the options. And, importantly, unlike in the sincerity framework of the khawaja sira, it doesn't stipulate that assignment to gender is valid for life. Instead, the law allows for change of one's gender identity once a year. Gender identity, according to the text of the German law, can be fluid and is not necessarily fixed. After all, everyone knows that *Empfindungen*, or sentiments, including the most deeply felt, can and do change. Love may turn into hate. Accordingly, feeling male may change into feeling female, and the possibility of frequent changes must therefore be legally supported. Such a dynamic gender identity is clearly not the gender identity of sincerity—it is the gender identity of profilicity.

The German law is about not just changing one's official gender status but also changing one's gendered name. One example given by the bill is the change of one's name from Marcus (male) to Angelika (female) and then, potentially, back to Marcus again.[66] The focus here is not on the gendered roles one needs to fulfill—for instance, in the family or on the job—but on how one is addressed and seen by others. The idea is not that when Marcus becomes Angelika she is expected to cook for her partner but that anyone, and especially people who do *not* know her personally—her university professor, let's say—must address her as Angelika and in this way confirm to her that she *is* a woman. The law is about mandating the *general peer*—any person or company or government agency—to do the same and to affirm her female identity. She then can *be* a woman, and dress and live as a woman, in any of the myriad ways one can dress and live as such. She can curate her female identity in accordance with the highly diverse options of being a woman today. In a profilic society, female profiles still differ from male profiles, but, unlike male and female gender roles, they differ in an unpredictable and nonhierarchical fashion.

All this goes to show that the purpose of the German law is not the promotion of the identity technology of authenticity. It does not emphasize turning away from social categories such as gender to find one's inner, original self beyond them. But it also does not promote the identity technology of sincerity, which builds selfhood in orientation to traditional gender roles. Instead, it promotes profilicity: the orientation to gendered profiles validated by a general peer—a validation that is manifested in the registration of a person's gender identity by the state.

Marcus is empowered by the law to self-determine that he is Angelika. The law mandates the state to register him as Angelika and, once this has happened, Angelika is a woman. It is assumed that for Angelika to be truly herself, the registration and validation of her female identity are essential. Being seen as a woman—assigned to the female gender and addressed in a feminine way—is the condition for her ability to build up true investment when she "presents herself to the world." In effect, what Angelika has self-determined is her gender profile.

To be clear, a legal reform regulating gender entries and their changes makes perfect sense in light of the main thesis of this book—namely, that gender identity has become profilic. There are different opinions on what such a law should look like exactly, and many of these have been expressed in the debate on the issue in the German parliament. Some argued that the proposed minimum age of fourteen to independently apply for a change of one's gender entry was too high.[67] Others said it was too low.[68] In any case, the fundamental problem remains that the legal document, like the public discourse it reflects, lacks a clear understanding of the very gender identity that it is supposed to regulate. Given this lack of clarity, it would make sense, as suggested in more detail in the conclusion of this book, to eliminate the gender entry altogether (a measure similar to removing religious affiliation from IDs) and to limit officially registered personal identity information to sex characteristics (similar to the biometric data now commonly included in IDs).

Unlike the presupposition in the German law, gender identity has never been and will never be straightforwardly self-determined by free will. There is also no specific age—fourteen or any other—at which an individual becomes fully autonomous to determine their gender identity "correctly." Profile curation, including gender profile curation, is part of an ongoing social-validation feedback loop. By cloaking itself in the mantle of authenticity, the German law obscures that it is in reality a law on gender *as* profile.

SARTRE, DE BEAUVOIR, AND MARX

Next to Hegel, another great star of the philosophy of authenticity was Jean-Paul Sartre. Sartre, of course, was also a prolific novelist and playwright. He expressed not only the ideas of the age of authenticity but also its feelings, its existential setting. One of his most famous quotes is "Hell is other people," a line from the play *No Exit*, written in 1944.[69]

"Hell is other people" can be taken to express a profound misanthropy, the mindset of a loner who cannot stand company. But Sartre explicitly rejected this interpretation: "It has been thought that what I meant by that was that our relations with other people are always poisoned, that they are invariably hellish relations."[70] This misunderstanding reflects a more general misunderstanding of authenticity—the idea that the authentic person is *so* original that she finds *everyone* else unoriginal, boring, and intolerable to be with and so ends up all alone as a miserable nihilist. This is a negative caricature of an authentic person—a caricature that reflects neither Sartre's philosophy nor his personality. The authentic person, instead, both enjoys and existentially needs company, other authentic people or, in popular language, "soulmates," fellow explorers of originality who can mutually recognize their authenticity. However, such soulmates are quite rare. Being unique is not for everybody.

Sartre explained the actual meaning of his famous catch-phrase in this way:

> I mean that if relations with someone else are twisted, vitiated, then that other person can only be hell. Why? Because . . . when we think about ourselves, when we try to know ourselves, . . . we use the knowledge of us which other people already have. We judge ourselves with the means other people have and have given us for judging ourselves. Into whatever I say about myself someone else's judgment always enters. Into whatever I feel within myself someone else's judgment enters.[71]

The suffering of the authentic person in the presence of "other people" refers to a situation—and these situations occur frequently in daily life—where one encounters not a soulmate but someone, maybe a colleague or family member, who, in one way or another, is prejudiced toward us and has certain expectations of us, typically because of our social identity, constituted by our roles. My boss may treat me not as me but as her employee. My father may treat me not as me but as his son. In such situations, we are forced to see ourselves, as Sartre says, constituted by "the knowledge of us which other people already have." In these cases, our sense of self is almost violently imposed on us "with the means other people . . . have given us for judging ourselves." Others force us to see ourselves as they see us. This existential situation poisons our authentic quest to find or create our true self: "Into whatever I feel within myself someone else's judgment enters." Once we are trapped in such inauthentic relationships, our pathway to becoming authentic is obstructed—we're condemned to remain inauthentic. There is no exit. We are in identity hell. "I am situating myself in a total dependence on someone else," Sartre concludes. "And then I am indeed in hell.

And there are a vast number of people in the world who are in hell because they are too dependent on the judgment of other people."[72]

When bemoaning the hellish dependance "on the judgment of other people," Sartre was still mainly thinking in terms of a regime of sincerity where people live mostly in the presence of role mates rather than soulmates—at home, at work, in church, in education, or in the military. The hell Sartre speaks of is a society where sincerity rules and where there is little room for authenticity. Sartre's purpose in writing books on authenticity—theoretical and literary ones—was to help spread the seed of authenticity, to create more authentic space in people's minds and in society, in the hope of eventually opening up emergency exits from the hell of sincerity.

Sartre himself did not live in sincerity hell, though. He was not just a part but a focal point of the hyperauthentic Parisian cultural elites of his time. He became an almost global symbol of the spirit of authenticity. He had a very special and nearly life-long soulmate, Simone de Beauvoir. The two, of course, never married—how could they, of all people, have embraced that core institution of sincerity that had long been serving the vicious function of transforming soulmates into role mates and preventing generation after generation of youths from ever becoming truly authentic? Marriage had been the traditional gateway to the hell of sincerity, and it too used to have no exit.

Sarte's existentialism is just as much de Beauvoir's existentialism. The two developed it together in their writings and in their lives. But de Beauvoir applied it in a way that turned out to be historically more influential and persistent—she related it to gender and thereby paved the way for a new, authentic form of feminism. She played a crucial role in transforming what is now called first-wave feminism into second-wave feminism by going beyond the demand for equal rights for women, such as voting or property rights. Grounded in her existentialist philosophical position, she questioned the very nature of gender and what it meant not just socially but also personally. Largely owing to her brilliant and comprehensive book *The Second Sex*, first published in 1949 in two volumes, nearly one thousand pages combined, the conceptual distinction between biologically constituted sex and socially constructed gender eventually became commonplace. This foundational insight is famously summarized in her proclamation "One is not born, but rather becomes, a woman."[73] The distinction between the sex one is born with and the gender one becomes in society remains until today a formative conceptual steppingstone that all gender debates, including those on transgender, must consider.

For practically all "classical" authors of authenticity, including de Beauvoir, authenticity arises out of the revolt against sincerity. But de Beauvoir realized much more clearly and deeply than her existentialist predecessors and collaborators how crucial and foundational the connection between sincerity on the one hand and sex and gender on the other had always been. From her perspective, the social roles that provided orientation for shaping a sincere identity had been first and foremost, and quite literally from the start (from birth onward), *gender* roles. For centuries, the practice of sincerity was built on gender, and gender was built on sincerity. Sincerity made use of the sexual differences between human beings, of the dualism between female and male bodies, to establish a social order consisting of an intricate and mostly hierarchical structure of distinctions between masculine and feminine. The modes of production, political hierarchies, the organization of kinship—all were designed along gender divisions. And all moral, religious, and ideological narratives, along with all artistic creations, served to celebrate, legitimize, or decree these divisions. Crucially, from an existentialist perspective, people had *internalized* them. Over millennia, sincere identity had been gendered.

For de Beauvoir—from a historical, political, and, most important, existential perspective—the authentic revolt against sincerity needed to be a revolt against the gendered self. The gendered self had not just been a side effect of the regime of sincerity; it was its biologically legitimized and behaviorally and psychologically internalized seed in every individual. To overcome sincerity, the gendered self had to be uprooted.

It is important to note that de Beauvoir, unlike many feminists of later waves, never questioned the biological distinctness of the sexes.[74] Her point had never been either to deny a connection between sex and gender—she was fully aware that social gender hierarchies had taken root so deeply precisely because they were propped up by biology—or to unrealistically demand that biological sex differences be somehow abolished. De Beauvoir was "sex positive," in a double sense: She affirmed the sexual characteristics of the human body as well as the use of these characteristics to achieve physical, emotional, and social pleasure. Inauthenticity, for her, was a result not of sex differences but of gender differences. Her call to thoroughly subvert the latter should not be misunderstood as a rejection of the former. Not least for the sake of sex, gender and sex had to be conceptually divorced. To be able to become authentically sexual, gender had to be critiqued. Sexual liberation was to be achieved over the dead body of gender hierarchy.

"Hell is other people" is a motto representing Sartre's take on authenticity. In *The Second Sex*, de Beauvoir quotes a remark by the American writer Dorothy Parker that sums up her own stance on the matter: "I cannot be just to books which treat of woman as woman. . . . My idea is that all of us, men as well as women, should be regarded as human beings."[75] Books that "treat of woman as woman" had been indoctrinatory instruments of patriarchal regimes of sincerity. They had seduced their female readers to internalize those depictions of "women as women" so that they eventually would also think of themselves *as women* rather than as simply humans. For de Beauvoir, "the fact is that every concrete human being is always a singular, separate individual."[76] This is to say, any individual is unique and original and can never be accurately identified by their gender. As long as women identify *as* women, they deny themselves their "sovereign individuality."[77]

For de Beauvoir, social and political revolution was needed to make genders equal and thereby to make gender (but not sex) differences irrelevant. Her existential feminism was strongly influenced by Marxism, and its logic resembles the Marxist logic of class struggle. The point of class struggle was to eliminate class hierarchies. It was not about enabling people to identify with their class status more happily but about *abolishing* classes altogether. Marx, too, was a thinker of the age of authenticity. He did not wish to idealize the working class and did not appeal to workers to internalize their class status. Yes, workers needed to understand the socioeconomic structures that, for the time being, condemned them to be proletarians. But the proletarian revolution, Marx hoped, would eventually lead to a classless society that would make it easier for everyone to live as authentic individuals, freed from any assignments to classes.

In an often-quoted passage from the first chapter of *The German Ideology*, Marx writes:

> As long . . . as activity is not voluntarily, but naturally, divided, man's own deed becomes an alien power opposed to him, which enslaves him instead of being controlled by him. For as soon as the distribution of labor comes into being, each man has a

particular, exclusive sphere of activity, which is forced upon him and from which he cannot escape. He is a hunter, a fisherman, a herdsman, or a critical critic, and must remain so if he does not want to lose his means of livelihood; while in communist society, where nobody has one exclusive sphere of activity but each can become accomplished in any branch he wishes, society regulates the general production and thus makes it possible for me to do one thing today and another tomorrow, to hunt in the morning, fish in the afternoon, rear cattle in the evening, criticize after dinner, just as I have a mind, without ever *becoming* hunter, fisherman, herdsman or critic.[78] (Emphasis added)

In effect, Marx presents an analysis of the regime of sincerity from a materialist perspective. He regards the mode of production—or, simply, the economy—as the defining force that conditions everything else in a society, including how people shape the sense of who they are. Accordingly, the roles he focuses on most are economic professions. The distribution of labor had resulted in literally "natural" economic roles: People were *born* into their trades as sons of hunters, sons of fishermen, and so on. These roles were inescapably forced on people. The only identity technology available to them, if they didn't want to lose their source of income, was to sincerely commit to their role: They had to *be* a hunter or a fisherman and *remain so* and therefore lived in a self-alienated state, lacking autonomy. Marx said of this kind of society that "what we ourselves produce" is turned "into an objective power above us, growing out of our control."[79] Our own productive work paradoxically becomes what takes away our subjective agency. What we do—that is, our profession—controls us; we do not express ourselves freely as individuals in what we do.

Communist society, Marx envisioned, would change this fundamentally. It would enable *everyone*—not just the property-owning capitalist minority—to "do one thing today and another tomorrow," as they saw fit. It would free people altogether from being *existentially defined* by their job. One could be a taxi driver in the morning and a blogger in the afternoon without ever *becoming* either. Marx hoped that communism would be the socioeconomic condition for switching one's identity technology from sincerity to authenticity. Each person would *be* a sovereign individual, a person in control of rather than controlled and *identified by* their work.

Although, at least to my knowledge, Marx never literally said, "One is not born, but rather becomes, a worker," the passage quoted above implies this very idea. The whole point of communism is to liberate workers—and everyone else, for that matter—from being forced to identify with their class or profession. De Beauvoir, in turn, at least as far as I know, never literally wrote, "I may clean the house in the morning, do construction work in the afternoon, put on make-up in the evening, and go to sleep with my girlfriend at night, just as I have a mind, without ever becoming a man or a woman." In any case, the whole point of feminism, for de Beauvoir, was to liberate women (and men) from being forced to *become* their "gender identity."

De Beauvoir wished to move beyond the assignment of individuals to gender identity—beyond that *Zuordnung* that the German bill on the self-determination of gender celebrates "as of outstanding importance for individual identity."

THE NASTY BITCHES

Alongside her passionate pleas to move beyond a fixation on gender identity and toward authentic selfhood, de Beauvoir expressed serious doubts that this goal could ever be achieved.

Since feminism and Marxism shared that same dream, she had hoped that communism might provide the conditions—that is, socioeconomic, political, and cultural equality—for authenticity to finally prevail. Alas, her hopes had been disappointed: The "new woman," she wrote, has appeared "nowhere, in Russia no more than in France or the United States."[80] Today, eight decades after *The Second Sex* was first published, authenticity is no longer a dream, but increasingly looks like a *simulacrum*—a copy of an original that never existed.[81] While its language strangely prevails, reality has moved decisively beyond it.

The fascination with the semantics of authenticity arose when sincerity waned. But the waning of fixed social roles, regarding both gender and the division of labor, by no means left the individuals all on their own, as authenticity had hoped. Instead, the waning of roles was accompanied by the waxing of profiles. And the shift from roles to profiles closely concerns gender.

Queens was a TV series that ran on the ABC network in the United States from October 2021 to May 2022.[82] Although discontinued after only one season, it received positive reviews. The rating platform Rotten Tomatoes shows a 100 percent approval rating, with an average rating of 8/10.[83] Wikipedia explains that the plot of the show revolves around an all-female music outfit who "once appeared as the 'Nasty Bitches' in the 1990s" and "turned the world of hip-hop upside down." Now they reunite, "but will the former megastars, also known as Professor Sex, Butter Pecan, Da Thrill and Xplicit Lyrics, manage to achieve this ambitious goal" of returning to their former fame and prestige?[84] As a trailer for the show, a music video featuring the song "Nasty Girl" was posted on YouTube.[85] Two days later, it had more than two million views.

The hip-hop video presents the four female stars in a fashion customary in this genre—displaying promiscuity and highlighting sexualized body parts, demonstrating individual wealth, consumerism, and a hedonistic lifestyle. Nothing in the videos portrays them in accordance with traditional female gender roles, such as wife, mother, or daughter. The first scene in which one of the group members appears shows her wearing a huge golden necklace identifying her as a "Nasty Bitch" and expressing her dismay at being addressed as "Ma'am." The traditional gender role-related designation is explicitly dismissed by her and implicitly replaced by the prominently displayed "cool" name of the group that supplies her with her profile. It is resoundingly clear that the Nasty Bitches do not conform or commit to traditional gender roles such as those described by de Beauvoir. And yet they hardly represent "sovereign individuality." Instead, they supply viewers with an attractive virtual gender profile.

At first sight it might seem that the Nasty Bitches represent the realization of the socioeconomic, cultural, and political equality of women that de Beauvoir envisioned as necessary for their transition to true authenticity. "Professor Sex" informs us first off that her "poom poom nani nani" (an allusion to her vagina) is "dripped in gold" and that "Ferraris fly me around the globe." All four women have fully emancipated themselves from male repression. In most scenes they socially or sexually dominate their male counterparts, who are depicted as male strippers. Butter Pecan explains: "Nasty women, we about nothin' but winnin.' It's money over men you never catchin' us slippin.'" To confirm that she has cast away the restrictions tied to traditional feminine gender roles of wife and mother and achieved independence, Xplicit Lyrics sings: "This is queen's madness rep my borough thorough as men. And when it comes to the paper they wanna borrow my pen." Xplicit Lyrics also points out that she crossed traditional racial boundaries with her talents: "I made a hit list, I'm a queen, young, black, and gifted."[86] However, the group members are not that young; after all, the show is about their second career after a hiatus of twenty years. Some of them show body weight that does not conform to earlier beauty standards according to which women were expected to be slim. In this way, the group also conveys defiance of ageism and gender-related bodily norms.

And yet, all this economic, political, and cultural equality for women hardly leads to the emergence of pure "sovereign individuality." From beginning to end, the iconography of the video focuses on a standardized "coolness" in the form of (dance) moves, gestures, and expressions highly familiar to most viewers of similar videos. The video promotes extreme consumerism and brand-consciousness through the display of luxury items and the mentioning of brand names in the lyrics: "I pull up with the Louis [Vuitton] luggage, I made it a set." Moreover, the video itself is not just a musical performance, not purely entertainment; it is a trailer for a TV series and so simultaneously advertises for the large media company ABC. In this hyper-capitalist context, the symbolic markers of equality and gender emancipation are commodified.

No one woman is born a Nasty Bitch; and it is not a gender role. But neither is a Nasty Bitch doing as de Beauvoir hoped authentic women would eventually do, "taking charge of her own existence" rather than succumbing to a gendered label.[87] Nasty Bitch is one of the many carefully curated gendered profiles presented and validated in the media. A woman can become a Nasty Bitch by curating her profile in alignment with what she sees when she watches *Queens* or any other of the countless similar media productions. But of course, she can just as well choose otherwise. And in any case, as the short rise and sudden fall of *Queens* demonstrates, you can never know when a profile may cease to be fully convincing.

INFLUENCERS

In 2021, nine of the top ten German social media influencers, in terms of market value, were women. This is according to a report in the online edition of the leading "quality newspaper" *Frankfurter Allgemeine Zeitung* (FAZ), which in turn cites a study, by the consulting firm Batten & Company and the market research firm Appinio, that analyzed data related to platforms such as Instagram, YouTube, and TikTok.[88] All nine female influencers at the top of the list focus on topics that have been associated with stereotypical women's interests: beauty, fashion, and fitness. To give readers an impression of the content they typically create, FAZ describes a scene from a viral video in which the presenter "throws a silver glitter handbag over her shoulder that perfectly matches her skirt and backless top. She then walks through a white double door to a window overlooking the Eiffel Tower, steps onto the balcony and poses by the window."

According to the FAZ story, male influencers tend to focus, albeit not always as profitably as their female counterparts, on "men's interests," such as computer games and motor sports. You do not have to be an identity theoretician to know that success for an influencer consists in the curation of an attractive profile. And the reported data suggest that the most successful profiles on social media are conspicuously gendered. But while gendering seems to be a necessary condition for making a social media profile truly valuable, it is not sufficient.

FAZ asks of the three women who lead the German influencer value rankings in 2021, What is the secret to their success? Well, of course, it is most useful that all three of the mentioned "women's interests"—beauty, fashion, and fitness—lend themselves quite naturally to advertising and product placement. They are easily monetizable and can make an influencer rich. But again, advertising and product placement alone are not that alluring to an audience; on the contrary, if not done in the right way they can be boring or off-putting. To make a profile really popular, and to make its audience sympathetic despite commodifying it for all to see, a very special quality is needed. The secret of success shared by Leonie Hanne, Pamela Reif, and Caro Daur, the top three German influencers, is . . .? You guessed it: their authenticity! "More than anything else, the authenticity of the three makes the difference," FAZ explains.

But wherein concretely lies the authenticity that gives the top influencers an edge over their competitors? According to FAZ:

> The women only accept advertising deals that fit their image. With lots of personal content from their everyday lives, they create closeness so that fans can identify particularly well with the accounts. A clear brand core results in performance promises that the influencers keep: Pamela Reif has workout videos and nutrition tips, Leonie Hanne and Caro Daur provide insights into trends and a world of luxury that is unattainable for many. A "consistent look and feel" rounds off the appearances.

The three women show true investment in their profiles by consistently presenting themselves in alignment with their personal brand, the integrity of which must be protected. At the same time, they make sure that what they do and how they look always resonates with their general peer, their millions of followers. As the FAZ report highlights, the crucial thing is that the audience can "identify particularly well with," and feel a certain "closeness" to, the curated profiles. It's a social-validation feedback loop: in their performances, the influencers identify "authentically" with their brand so that the viewers can "authentically" identify with it as well, and both sides thereby mutually confirm and deepen the "authenticity" of their identities.

When applied to popular influencers, the notion of authenticity may raise suspicion. How can something so obviously staged, so blatantly conformist, and so unapologetically commercial be labeled "authentic?" How can this concept, of all things, be named by both an empirical market study and a quality journalism outlet as the "secret" at the heart of contemporary social media personalities? At least at first sight, however, one might ask whether the marketing firm and the journalist might be correct. Why question, from the outside, the free will and self-determination of Leonie Hanne, Pamela Reif, or Caro Daur in choosing who they are and, accordingly, presenting their true selves to the world? Why doubt the authenticity of their focus on their gender identities when they express themselves in emphatically feminine ways?

From the perspective of this book, however, using the language of authenticity to explain the success of influencers is a variation of the semantic and conceptual confusion depicted in the preceding pages. In transgender and cisgender alike, in law and in politics, in medicine and in social media, we are still enthralled by a deep nostalgia for authenticity. It seems that, against all evidence, we want to prove to ourselves that we are still authentic or, even better, more authentic than we have ever been. Perhaps we praise as authentic the presumably true investment made by Hanne, Reif, and Daur in their identities because we wish to convince ourselves that we, too, can still be authentic when we curate our own profiles in a manner not all that different from theirs.

TEN THESES ON GENDER

What follows from these observations, analyses, and descriptions of gender, including transgender, today? Here are ten theses:

1. Gender identity today is often no longer a role identity but a profile identity. Along with the general shift toward profilicity as a dominant identity technology, gender identity, which continues to be central to the sense of self, is now increasingly profilic as well.

2. In profilicity, we present gendered profiles of ourselves and build true investment in them through social-validation feedback loops. Natalie Wynn defines gender expression as a "style,"[89] explaining that we present ourselves in a gendered way "to prompt others to see us for what we are."[90] When our "gender style" is publicly appreciated, we can identify with it. That's profilicity.

3. Gender matters again. During the age of authenticity, gender tended to be regarded as secondary to human individuality. Gender was seen, especially by feminists, as a social construct creating inequality between the sexes, imposing conformity, and establishing hierarchical roles. The point was to overcome the internalization of gender roles and the hierarchies they established, to enable everyone to become original and free. In profilicity, however, gender is once more regarded as central to human identity. It cannot be discarded and must be displayed.

4. Transgender is at the forefront of the present shift toward gender as profile. Transgender is no longer at the fringes but has

a strong presence in media, politics, law, academia, and culture. It has become a valid alternative to the male–female binary. In transgender today, gendered self-presentation and public validation of one's gender identity is emphasized—thereby, it differs from authenticity. But while transgender today stresses the presentation of a person's gender, it clearly does not promote traditional gender roles. As it is lived today, transgender is the most obviously profilic gender.

5. While transgender today is arguably the avant-garde of the shift to profilic gender, cisgender, too, has become highly profilic. Influencers and pop culture present a plethora of still mostly cisgendered profiles. The public presentation and validation of gender profiles is equally characteristic of cisgender and transgender today.

6. Everybody must get gendered. In profilicity, where gender is "style," no one escapes gendering. No-style is also a style. Nonbinary or other "noncommitted" gender identities are nonetheless gender identities.

7. We look at profilic gender through the rearview mirror of authenticity. Although gender has become increasingly profilic, we still use the outdated vocabulary of authenticity to describe it. We haven't yet developed a semantics of profilicity. This causes confusion and contradictions. In particular, it fosters the gender metaphysics and theology of gender-essence theories, the myth of the wrong body, and the idea that the true self must get its gender right in order to be whole and happy.

8. Gender identity cannot be self-determined—it is relational and contingent. A confusing effect of the inappropriate use of authenticity language to describe gender as profile is the counterfactual assumption that gender ought to be self-determined. It is logically contradictory to state that a person's gender is not their choice and that they therefore ought to autonomously decide

what their gender is. What is more, one's sense of self—one's identity, including one's gender identity—is established by making use of socially and culturally embedded identity technologies. Identity, including any gender identity, is always already, and has always been, socially conditioned in conjunction with a person's biology and psychology, which are also not self-determined.

9.   Projecting the language of authenticity onto transgender is not helpful. While transgender is at the forefront of the shift to gender as profile, it is also particularly exposed to problematic authenticity claims. The media frame transgender in traditional authenticity narratives of "finding one's true self." Medicine markets gender-affirming procedures as authenticity-enhancing. The law stipulates that transgender legislation serves the promotion of autonomous individuality. Transgender people have been expected to demonstrate their authenticity when going to a public restroom. In a sense, society has projected onto transgender people its futile attempt to save authenticity in times of profilicity. They are given the task of assuring everyone that we can, contradictorily, still be authentic as we curate our profiles.

10.   Profilic gender is beyond good and evil. There is nothing wrong with profilic gender identities as such, whether cis- or transgender. Profilic gender is non-authentic and non-sincere, but also neither inauthentic nor insincere. It is neither more nor less valuable or true than gender identity under conditions of sincerity or authenticity. In modern society, traditionally sincere roles have become largely obsolete. The contradictions of authenticity gave rise to its gradual demise as well. Profilicity reflects today's highly dynamic and highly mediated and digitalized society where profiles, or identity brands, have become ubiquitous. It is no wonder, then, that gender has also become profilic. But any identity technology has its risks, dangers, and pathologies.

People can be overinvested in their profiles, just as they can be overcommitted to their roles or obsessed with their pursuit of originality. In today's neoliberal and hyper-capitalist world, profiles lend themselves to extreme commodification and exhibition. They can easily be instrumentalized for ideological agendas. This is also the case for (trans-)gender profiles. It is important to avoid overinvestment in one's profiles and to remain at ease even when one doesn't achieve the validation one may have hoped for. Identity, including gender identity, is always ultimately incoherent and incongruent, no matter which identity technology we use to construct it.

CONCLUSION

Before this book was written, Jared Morningstar, a reader of *You and Your Profile*, formulated one of its main ideas in a short piece on the online platform Medium.[1] Applying the identity technologies sincerity, authenticity, and profilicity to gender, Morningstar wrote:

> In sincerity, gender is expressed simply through adherence to gender roles given to you, and in authenticity, gender is experienced through true inner feelings unique to your individuality (which is absolutely how a lot of people DO primarily experience gender—these different technologies are not necessarily mutually exclusive and authenticity is still prominent, even as profilicity is on the rise). But in profilicity, gender identity becomes primarily a phenomenon of feeling satisfied with how you believe you are being perceived by the general peer—it becomes a question of how you are seen by others, not simply how you understand and perceive yourself in accordance with some authentic inner reality.[2]

Morningstar clearly pointed out a core difference between this approach to identity (and gender) and the heated political debates about these issues today: it is not normative. He correctly stated that I am not "trying to claim that any of these identity technologies are good or bad in themselves, or that any of them are somehow more effective at creating 'real' identity." Just as none of the three identity technologies is more or less correct per se, none of the gender identities constructed with their help gets gender more or less right. Each identity technology is embedded in social and historical circumstances that make the respective types of gender work and seem plausible.

Three basic (but also somewhat complex) conclusions from understanding gender through identity technologies are as follows. First, contrary to what is often suggested today, as in the German law on the self-determination of gender, gender identity is never and can never be *autonomously determined* by supposedly sovereign individuals. Gender identity is not hidden somewhere deep down in the self and then discovered through personal introspection. Instead, one's sense of self and gender develops in a manner that is contingent on the identity technologies available and practiced in the society in which one lives. It is contingent also on the biological and psychological circumstances that characterize a person—that is, on one's body and mind.

Second, there is no perfect fit between one's sex and biology, their complex, changing, and often contradictory thoughts and feelings, and their various and varying social relationships and positions. How one is feminine, masculine, or transgender involves dissonance and instability. To make such incongruities bearable, or to cover them up, is a prime function of identity technologies. By means of sincere role commitment, the pursuit of originality, or true investment in their profiles, a person can form a seemingly coherent and credible sense of self and gender.

Third, given the differences between the various identity technologies and the social, cultural, and historical contexts in which they function, *being* male, female, or transgender has different and often incompatible meanings for different individuals at different times and in different places. Being a hijra in India or being a burrnesha in Albania are very different forms of being third gender under different regimes of sincerity. In turn, these third gender identities differ quite radically from what it means to be a transgender person under conditions of profilicity. The differences are so drastic that a third gender person and a person identifying as transgender may mutually reject the lifestyle of the other.

There is a peculiar difference between sincere and profilic gender identity on the one hand and authentic gender identity on the other. Under conditions of both sincerity and profilicity, it matters a lot which particular gender one is. In authenticity, however, gender identity is regarded as secondary to individuality and uniqueness. Here, a person pursues originality—and gender is always somewhat unoriginal. It is perceived as a general and anonymous categorization, an impersonal label imposed on individuals from the outside. It smacks of conformity and commitment to gender roles, or it is suspected of giving rise to narcissist and inauthentic gendered self-profiling—for instance, in the form of cosmetic surgery or bodybuilding.

In an essay in the popular philosophical magazine *Philosophy Now*, Thorsten Botz-Bornstein asks what a Daoist sage might have to say about gender and identity politics today.[3] He suggests that, from a Daoist point of view, "identities and genders are produced by our ways of behaving and our ways of seeing while we are living in cultures." This sounds reasonable to me. As does the following claim: "Daoism wouldn't make statements about fixed gender essences or about the linguistic rules linked to these essences. Daoism would [recognize that] all things are . . . in constant flow."[4] Stipulating that a Daoist would maintain "that fixed gender identity simply does not matter," Botz-Bornstein then concludes that "a Daoist sage would likely hold that an individual cannot be defined through gender, and that therefore, gender identity cannot be reduced to names or pronouns."[5] About this, I am not so sure.

The position on gender and gendered pronouns that Botz-Bornstein ascribes to the Daoist sage eventually sounds to me more like that of an adherent of the age of authenticity. When he writes that "an *individual* cannot be *defined* through gender" (emphasis added) and claims that (gender) identity is irreducible to pronouns, he evokes, intentionally or not, core tropes of the age of authenticity: Everything is about individuality, and this individuality is so unique and original that gender cannot define it and language cannot express it—especially not gendered language. In effect, Botz-Bornstein here reiterates a modern understanding of Daoism as individualism.

In my understanding, Daoism does recognize that gender identity matters—precisely because there is no essential self underneath. From the somewhat paradoxical perspective of genuine pretending, gender identities are pretended—that is performed, played, relational, and contingent, and thereby able to genuinely define who one is, if only temporarily. Daoism, as I see it, is not about the true individual beyond any "fixed gender." It is about dealing productively with the contingencies one encounters and cannot avoid, including the contingencies of one's gender.

This being said, I sympathize with Botz-Bornstein's (implicitly) authentic take on gender identity. He and I are of the same generation and from the same country; we are both children of the age of authenticity. While acknowledging the Daoist insight into the existential condition of genuine pretending, I tend to find my personal genuineness in the mode of authenticity. This means that I too tend to regard my gender as secondary, as not really definitive of who I uniquely am. To me, too, pronouns seem to be not really a big deal—they are a superficial language convention that cannot reach my inner self. But then again, insight into genuine pretending has led me to understand that this kind of gender identity suits me just fine, owing to where and when I happened to grow up, but that it does not necessarily suit everyone else. The Daoist diver in the story from the *Zhuangzi* grew up near the water and got comfortable with it. I grew up in the age of authenticity, and eventually managed to make myself reasonably comfortable therein.

Younger generations today grow up in the presence of profilicity, and they need to get comfortable with it. Their approach to their gender identities needs to be different from that of people like Botz-Bornstein or me. Under conditions of profilicity, gender is part of a person's profile(s) and must be curated—and the options available for gender curation have now been extended beyond the traditional male–female binary. Profilic transgender, in many variations, has become a valid alternative to an authentic attitude to gender. "This isn't at all to say that people who come to trans identity under conditions of profilicity are somehow less genuine as a result," Jared Morningstar writes, "but rather that a proliferation of transgender and non-binary identities is simply an outcome of profilicity, just how certain modes of being rose to greater prominence when authenticity came on the scene (heterodox thinkers, hopeless romantics, and visionary artists being some examples)." He continues: "If authenticity is an inner alchemy of pure self-discovery, then profilicity is an alchemy of perception and appearances. In that way,

profilicity is more social, contextual, and immediately connected with a world outside of an atomized individual, which
has some benefits."⁶ Yes, this is how it seems to me, too.

What does all of this mean practically? How can an understanding of gender as profile help solve current issues about
transgender people and their rights? To end this book, here's a
concrete suggestion regarding the new German law on the self-
determination of gender: The difference between gender and
biological sex should be made more explicit. The German language still lacks a clear terminological distinction between sex
and gender—both are *Geschlecht*. It would make sense to officially register a person's biological characteristics rather than
their gender identity and to specify that only the former and not
the latter are entered onto an ID or passport. In addition to other
bodily features (e.g., fingerprints, blood type) and biometrical
data that are officially recorded to identify or characterize
individuals, there could be an entry on specific sexually relevant
features, e.g., gametes.

Gender differentiations, however, across society do not need
to be made according to only one fixed general standard and
could be treated pragmatically. In different contexts, different
distinctions between genders can apply. Public bathrooms are
now increasingly unisex and can thereby be accessible to all genders alike. Where nudity is common (e.g., saunas), there may be
provisions to create both inclusive (unisex) and exclusive spaces
for people with different genital features and genders, depending on preferences and demand. In sports, it makes sense (for
sporting reasons) to continue traditional divisions between male
and female competitions based on biology at birth. However,
gender categories in sports may be extended beyond binary
distinctions to accommodate transgender athletes. Gender
"self-determination" in the sense of self-categorization can be

practiced in many other contexts, such as on dating apps. Here, a multitude of gender designations is already available. Users may be given options to indicate not only their gender identities but also their bodily features. A person may identify as male and state that he has a vagina in order to inform the expectations of potential partners. Last but not least, a more flexible and less metaphysical or ideological approach to gender identity may prevent people from overidentifying with their genders and enable them to be more at ease with them.

NOTES

INTRODUCTION

1. Lydia Polgreen, host, *The Ezra Klein Show*, "We Need Better Narratives About Gender," podcast, produced by Kristin Lin, October 10, 2023, YouTube, 1:05:49, https://www.youtube.com/watch?v=h4PVn7_BX0Q. All the following quotes from Lydia Polgreen and Masha Gessen are from this source.
2. Miquel Missé, *The Myth of the Wrong Body* (Cambridge: Polity Press, 2022).
3. Missé, *Wrong Body*, 18.
4. Missé, *Wrong Body*, 16
5. Missé, *Wrong Body*, 20.
6. Missé, *Wrong Body*, 31–32.
7. Missé, *Wrong Body*, 31
8. Missé, *Wrong Body*, 31.
9. Missé, *Wrong Body*, 16.
10. Missé, *Wrong Body*, 17.
11. Missé, *Wrong Body*, 9.
12. Missé, *Wrong Body*, 30, emphasis in the original.
13. Missé, *Wrong Body*, 26.
14. Missé, *Wrong Body*, 14.
15. Missé, *Wrong Body*, 33.
16. Missé, *Wrong Body*, 33.
17. Missé, *Wrong Body*, 23.

18. Missé, *Wrong Body*, 111–12.

19. Missé, *Wrong Body*, 116.

20. Missé, *Wrong Body*, 112.

21. Missé, *Wrong Body*, x, emphasis in the original.

22. Missé, *Wrong Body*, 138.

23. Missé, *Wrong Body*, 127.

24. Hans-Georg Moeller and Paul J. D'Ambrosio, *You and Your Profile: Identity After Authenticity* (New York: Columbia University Press, 2021).

25. See Moeller and D'Ambrosio, *You and Your Profile*.

26. Lionel Trilling, *Sincerity and Authenticity* (Cambridge, MA: Harvard University Press, 1972).

27. Charles Taylor, *A Secular Age* (Cambridge, MA: Harvard University Press, 2007).

28. For a definition of "profilicity," see my YouTube video "Profilicity: The Definition" at *Carefree Wandering*, February 3, 2025, 12:38, https://www.youtube.com/watch?v=fk2PpmlxIfA.

I. A DAOIST VIEW ON GENDER AND IDENTITY

1. *The School of Life*, "Eastern Philosophy—Lao Tzu," YouTube video, 10:02, November 21, 2014, https://www.youtube.com/watch?v=dFb7Hxva5rg; I critiqued this video on my channel *Carefree Wandering*, "Critique of Eastern Philosophy—Lao Tzu," YouTube video, 26:00, March 17, 2021, https://www.youtube.com/watch?v=O3y7aiwp4sY.

2. See, e.g., Ronnie Littlejohn, "Daoist Philosophy," in *Internet Encyclopedia of Philosophy*, https://iep.utm.edu/daoismdaoist-philosophy/.

3. The most famous version of this story appears in the historical text *Shiji*, or *Records of the Grand Historian*, which dates to the second century BCE (see *Shiji*:63). If not indicated otherwise, early Chinese sources are cited with reference to the online database *Chinese Text Project*, https://ctext.org/. If not indicated otherwise, translations are mine.

4. See John Makeham, *Name and Actuality in Early Chinese Thought* (Albany: SUNY Press, 1994).

5. *Analects* (*Lunyu*), 13:3.

6. *Analects* (*Lunyu*), 12:11.

7. *Hanfeizi* 7:2, in *Han Feizi: Basic Writings*, trans. Burton Watson (New York: Columbia University Press, 1964), 32.

8. As it occurs, for instance, in *Thus Spoke Zarathustra*, 4:61; accessed from the online database Nietzsche Source, http://www.nietzschesource.org /#eKGWB.

9. See Paul D'Ambrosio, Hans-Rudolf Kantor, and Hans-Georg Moeller, "Incongruent Names: A Theme in the History of Chinese Philosophy," *Dao: A Journal of Comparative Philosophy* 17, no. 3 (2018): 305–30.

10. See my interpretation and translation of the first chapter of the *Laozi* in Hans-Georg Moeller, *Dao De Jing* (Chicago: Open Court, 2007), 3–5.

11. See the chapter "Paradox Politics" in Hans-Georg Moeller, *The Philosophy of the Daodejing* (New York: Columbia University Press, 2006), 55–74.

12. Brook Ziporyn, *Zhuangzi: The Complete Writings* (Indianapolis: Hackett, 2020), 47–48. Translation modified.

13. Ziporyn, *Zhuangzi*, 160. Translation modified.

14. *Zhuangzi*, 18:5; *Zhuangzi*, 1:4.

15. *Zhuangzi*, 6:7.

16. See *Analects* (*Lunyu*), 17:21.

17. Today's Confucian philosophers often disagree with this and other moral norms of early Confucianism that are not in line with contemporary ethical expectations.

18. *Mencius*, trans. D. C. Lau (London: Penguin, 1970), 190.

19. Hilary Whiteman, "Ballerina's Parents Jailed for Neglecting the Daughter They Bathed in Attention but Starved of Food," CNN, February 15, 2025, https://edition.cnn.com/2025/02/15/australia/australia -malnourished-girl-neglect-hnk-intl/index.html.

20. Ziporyn, *Zhuangzi*, 61.

21. Ziporyn, *Zhuangzi*, 62.

22. Ziporyn, *Zhuangzi*, 62.

23. Ziporyn, *Zhuangzi*. 11.

24. Ziporyn, *Zhuangzi*, 171.

25. I use quotation marks here because the technical term "metaphysics" stems from Greek philosophy and has no exact equivalent in the Chinese language.

26. *Zhuangzi*, 2:14.

27. See the English translation of selected commentaries on the story in Ziporyn, *Zhuangzi*, 162–63.

28. Hans-Georg Moeller, "Zhuangzi's Dream of a Butterfly: A Daoist Interpretation," *Philosophy East and West* 49 (1999): 439–450; and *Daoism Explained: From the Dream of the Butterfly to the Fishnet Allegory* (Chicago: Open Court, 2004).

29. Herbert A. Giles, *Chuang Tzu: Mystic, Moralist, and Social Reformer* (London: Bernard Quaritch, 1889), https://www.gutenberg.org/files /59709/59709-h/59709-h.htm.

30. James Legge, *The Sacred Books of China: The Texts of Taoism* (Oxford: Clarendon Press, 1891), https://ctext.org/dictionary.pl?if=en&id=2732; Martin Buber, *Reden und Gleichnisse des Tschuang-Tse* (Leipzig: Insel, 1921), 9.

31. *Zhuangzi*, 6:5.

32. Unfortunately, several Western translations of the story suggest that Zhuangzi remembers his dream after waking up and is then in a state of confusion about reality and illusion. This, I argue, is a misinterpretation. See Moeller, "Zhuangzi's Dream of a Butterfly," 439–50.

33. For an illustration of the scene, see Lu Zhi's sixteenth-century depiction in "*Zhuangzi* (book)," Wikipedia, accessed March 1, 2025, https:// commons.wikimedia.org/wiki/File:Dschuang-Dsi-Schmetterling straum-Zhuangzi-Butterfly-Dream.jpg.

34. *Zhuangzi* 17:13; Hans-Georg Moeller, "Rambling Without Destination: On Daoist You-ing in the World," in *Zhuangzi and the Happy Fish*, ed. Roger T. Ames and Takahiro Nakajima (Honolulu: University of Hawaii Press, 2015), 248–60.

35. For an example of a visual representation, see Jin Tingbiao's eighteenth-century painting Hao Liang Tu (濠梁图, Illustration of the Hao-River story): https://catalog.digitalarchives.tw/item/00/15/27/3d.html.

36. E. N. Anderson, "Flowering Apricot: Environmental Practice, Folk Religion, and Daoism," in *Daoism and Ecology: Ways Within a Cosmic Landscape*, ed. N. J. Girardot et al. (Cambridge, MA: Harvard University Press, 2001), 278, quoted in Lisa Kemmerer, *Animals and World Religions* (New York: Oxford University Press, 2012), 161.

37. Anderson, "Flowering Apricot," 286.

38. *Mengzi*, 3A:4.

39. Lau, *Mencius*, 102.

40. Lau, *Mencius*, 102.

41. Lau, *Mencius*, 102.

42. For a fuller discussion of early Confucian "human supremacy" and its Daoist critique, see Hans-Georg Moeller, "Early Confucian 'Human Supremacy' and Its Daoist Critique," *Asian Studies* 11, no. 3 (2023): 71–92, https://doi.org/10.4312/as.2023.11.3.71-92.

43. *Xunzi*, 5:5.

44. *Xunzi*, 9:19.

45. *Zhuangzi*, 29:1.

46. A. C. Graham, *Chuang Tzu: The Inner Chapters* (Indianapolis: Hackett, 2001), 234.

47. Hans-Georg Moeller, "Gangster Zhi: Comedic Daoist Philosophical Practice," *Journal of Chinese Philosophy* 50, no. 1 (2023): 17–27.

48. Hans-Georg Moeller, "Kill Stories: A Critical Narrative in the Zhuangzi," *Dao: A Journal of Comparative Philosophy*, June 29, 2023, https://doi.org/10.1007/s11712-023-09892-w.

49. *Zhuangzi*, 9:1.

50. *Zhuangzi*, 9:3.

51. Zhuangzi 20:8; For an animated interpretation of this story, see my video at *Philosophy in Motion*, "Daoist Philosophy: Identity | Zhuangzi's The Hunt," July 7 2021, YouTube, 12:10, https://www.youtube.com/watch?v=wpAKbcPWhgE.

52. *Zhuangzi*, 18:5.

53. Ziporyn, *Zhuangzi*, 3.

54. Ziporyn, *Zhuangzi*, 5.

55. Ziporyn, *Zhuangzi*, 5.

56. Ziporyn, *Zhuangzi*, 7.

57. Hans-Georg Moeller and Paul D'Ambrosio, *Genuine Pretending: On the Philosophy of the Zhuangzi* (New York: Columbia University Press, 2017).

58. Henry Rosemont Jr., *Against Individualism: A Confucian Rethinking of the Foundations of Morality, Politics, Family, and Religion* (Lanham, MD: Lexington Books, 2015).

59. Rosemont, *Against Individualism*, 14.

60. Ziporyn, *Zhuangzi*, 111.

61. *Dadai Liji*, 38:11.

62. *Zhuangzi*, 14:6; Ziporyn, *Zhuangzi*, 124–25.

63. Ziporyn, *Zhuangzi*, 125.

64. *Zhuangzi*, 2:11. Ziporyn, *Zhuangzi*, 19.

65. See "Daoist Philosophy: Right & Wrong | Zhuangzi's Owls and Crows Crave Mice," an animated illustration and interpretation of this story on my channel *Philosophy in Motion*, April 24, 2021, YouTube, 12:00, https://www.youtube.com/watch?v=yEaPfVCUr2A.

66. Robin R. Wang, *Yinyang: The World of Heaven and Earth in Chinese Thought and Culture* (New York: Cambridge University Press, 2012), 6.

67. Wang, *Yinyang*, 5.

68. Wang, *Yinyang*, 5.

69. Wang, *Yinyang*, 24.

70. Stephan Feuchtwang, "Chinese Religions," in *Religions in the Modern World: Traditions and Transformations*, ed. Linda Woodhead, Christopher Partridge, and Hiroko Kawanami (New York: Routledge, 2016), 143–72, 150.

71. Wang, *Yinyang*, 7, quoting Alfred Forke, *The World-Conception of the Chinese: Their Astronomical, Cosmological, and Physico-Philosophical Speculations* (London: Arthur Probsthain, 1925), 215.

72. Wang, *Yinyang*, 8–11.

73. *Laozi*, 61, 28.

2. A SHORT THEORY OF THE SELF
AND ITS GENDER

1. Within the yinyang horizon, the dominant (but by no means only) conception of "the" soul (*hun-po* 魂魄) in China is dual and consists of a yin (*po*) and yang (*hun*) component. See, e.g., Farzeen Baldrian-Hussein, "Hun and Po 魂·魄: Yang Soul(s) and Yin Soul(s); Celestial Soul(s) and Earthly Soul(s)," in *The Encyclopedia of Taoism*, ed. Fabrizio Pregadio (London: Routledge, 2008), 521–23.

2. Plato, *The Republic of Plato*, trans. Allan Bloom (New York: Basic Books, 1991), 297–303, referencing *Republic* 614b–620d.

3. Benjamin Cabe, "On Gender and the Soul," *Theoria: Orthodox Christian Faith and Culture*, October 29, 2022, https://theoriatv.substack.com/p/on-gender-and-the-soul. *Consensus patrum* means the common view among the church fathers.

4. Cyril of Jerusalem, "Catechetical Lecture 4: On the Ten Points of Doctrine," *New Advent*, accessed March 10, 2025, https://www.newadvent.org/fathers/310104.htm.

5. Brian Hebblethwaite, *Philosophical Theology and Christian Doctrine* (Wiley Blackwell, 2005), 113.

6. Genesis 2:21–24, New American Bible, accessed July 20, 2025, https://www.vatican.va/archive/ENG0839/__P4.HTM.

7. Niklas Luhmann, "Frauen, Männer, und George Spencer Brown," *Zeitschrift für Soziologie* 17, no. 1 (1988): 47–71, quote from 51.

8. Luhmann, "Frauen, Männer," 47.

9. Immanuel Kant, "An Answer to the Question: What Is Enlightenment?," trans. Ted Humphrey (Hackett, 1992), https://www.nypl.org/sites/default/files/kant_whatisenlightenment.pdf, 1.

10. Kant, *What Is Enlightenment?*, 1.

11. Kant, *What Is Enlightenment?*, 1.

12. Luhmann, "Frauen, Männer," 53.

13. Luhmann, "Frauen, Männer," 47.

14. Natalie Wynn, "Autogynephilia," *ContraPoints*, February 2, 2018, YouTube, 15:14–15:18, https://www.youtube.com/watch?v=6czRFLs5JQo.

15. "Das: Ich denke, muss alle meine Vorstellungen begleiten können," in *Kritik der reinen Vernunft* (Critique of Pure Reason), B 131.

16. Jessica L. Tracy and Richard W. Robins, "Putting the Self Into Self-Conscious Emotions: A Theoretical Model," *Psychological Inquiry* 15, no. 2 (April 2004): 103–25; quote from 106, https://doi.org/10.1207/s15327965pli1502_01.

17. James J. Ponzetti, ed., *International Encyclopedia of Marriage and Family*, 2nd ed. (New York: Macmillan Reference USA, 2003), 728–29.

18. John Eccles, *Evolution of the Brain: Creation of the Self* (New York: Routledge, 1989); John Eccles, *How the Self Controls Its Brain* (New York: Springer-Verlag, 1994); Robert Sapolsky, *Determined: A Science of Life Without Free Will* (Penguin, 2023), 217.

19. Sapolsky, *Determined*, 1.

20. Sapolsky, *Determined*, 292.

21. The association of mind with power and control reappears in today's discourses about the potential dangers of so-called artificial intelligence. Here, algorithms or large language models are often described as not just metaphorically but literally intelligent—although they clearly do not have a mind and function by thoughtlessly processing data mostly by statistical means (see Elena Esposito, *Kommunikation mit unverständlichen Maschinen* [Vienna: Residenz Verlag, 2024]). In line with the logic of the traditional mind–body dualism, it is sometimes proposed that these programs may take over control of anything that is supposedly less "intelligent" than they, including humans, and potentially even become sentient and develop a self (see, e.g., Kartik Hosanagar, *A Human's Guide to Machine Intelligence: How Algorithms Are Shaping Our Lives and How We Can Stay in Control* [New York: Viking, 2019]).

22. Natalie Wynn, "Twilight," *ContraPoints*, March 2, 2024, YouTube, ca. 2:45:00, https://www.youtube.com/watch?v=bqloPw5wp48.

23. Wynn, "Twilight."

24. Wynn, "Twilight."

25. Scott Barry Kaufman, "Taking Sex Differences in Personality Seriously," *Scientific American*, December 12, 2019, accessed March 20, 2024, https://www.scientificamerican.com/blog/beautiful-minds/taking-sex-differences-in-personality-seriously/.

26. Kaufman, "Taking Sex Differences."

27. See, e.g., Andrew Lear and Eva Cantarella, *Images of Ancient Greek Pederasty: Boys Were Their Gods* (London: Routledge, 2009).

28. See Kenneth J. Dover, *Greek Homosexuality* (Cambridge, MA: Harvard University Press, 1978).

29. Brooke Sopelsa, "Nearly 30% of Gen Z Women Identify as LGBTQ, Gallup Survey Finds," NBC News, March 13, 2024, accessed March 10, 2025, https://www.nbcnews.com/news/us-news/nearly-30-gen-z-women-identify-lgbtq-gallup-survey-finds-rcna143019.

30. Luhmann, "Frauen, Männer," 49.

31. *Zhuangzi*, 19:10.

32. Brook Ziporyn, *Zhuangzi: The Complete Writings* (Indianapolis: Hackett, 2020), 154.

3. BEYOND THE WEST:
FROM GENDER ROLES TO PROFILES

1. Francis Fukuyama, *The End of History and the Last Man* (New York: Free Press, 1992).

2. C. Textor, "Urban and Rural Population of China from 2014 to 2024," Statista, January 17, 2025, https://www.statista.com/statistics/278566 /urban-and-rural-population-of-china/.

3. Kenneth Pletcher, "Consequences of China's One-Child Policy," *Britannica*, February 5, 2025, https://www.britannica.com/topic/one-child -policy/Consequences-of-Chinas-one-child-policy.

4. Michael Kwan, "What Killed Marriage? China's Divorce Rate Is up 75% in a Decade," December 2, 2021, https://www.ceibs.edu/new -papers-columns/20503.

5. Felix Richter, "Not Married, No Kids," Statista, November 10, 2023, https://www.statista.com/chart/31238/marriage-and-birth-rate-in -china/.

6. "China Fertility Rate (1950–2025)," Macrotrends, accessed March 11, 2025, https://www.macrotrends.net/global-metrics/countries/CHN /china/fertility-rate.

7. Richter, "Not Married."

8. Kwan, "Marriage."

9. Premchand Dommaraju and Gavin Jones, "Divorce Trends in Asia," *Asian Journal of Social Science* 39, no. 6 (2011): 725–50, https://doi.org/10 .1163/156853111X619201.

10. Tomás Sobotka, "World's Highest Childlessness Levels in East Asia," *Population & Societies* 2021/11, no. 595 (December 2021): 1–4, https:// doi.org/10.3917/popsoc.595.0001.

11. "Hello Kitty," Wikipedia, March 1, 2025, https://en.wikipedia.org/wiki /Hello_Kitty.

12. Esther Walker, "Top Cat: How 'Hello Kitty' Conquered the World," *Independent*, May 21, 2008, https://www.independent.co.uk/news/world /asia/top-cat-how-hello-kitty-conquered-the-world-831522.html.

13. Melanie L. Glocker et al., "Baby Schema in Infant Faces Induces Cuteness Perception and Motivation for Caretaking in Adults," *Ethology* 115, no. 3 (2009): 257–263, https://doi.org/10.1111/j.1439-0310.2008.01603.x.

14. Walker, "Top Cat."

15. Natalia Konstantinovskaia, "Being Kawaii in Japan," UCLA Center for the Study of Women, July 21, 2017, https://csw.ucla.edu/2017/07/21/being-kawaii-in-japan/.

16. Konstantinovskaia, "Kawaii."

17. Simon May, *The Power of Cute* (Princeton, NJ: Princeton University Press, 2019), 95.

18. May, *Cute*, 40.

19. May, *Cute*, 159

20. May, *Cute*, 163

21. May, *Cute*, 164.

22. A video of the interview has been personally shared by Fa and Hansen. Both gave their permission to quote from the interview.

23. Irene Tu, "Big 'They' Energy," *Don't Tell Comedy*, October 12, 2023, YouTube, 10:47, https://www.youtube.com/watch?v=GKcUe-LbYSY.

24. On the discourse about Asian Values, see Chang Yau Hoon, "Revisiting the Asian Values Argument Used by Asian Political Leaders and Its Validity," *Indonesian Quarterly* 32, no. 2 (2004): 154–74.

25. Geert Hofstede, *Culture's Consequences: Comparing Values, Behaviors, Institutions, and Organizations Across Nations*, 2nd ed. (Thousand Oaks, CA: Sage, 2001).

26. L. Beatrice, "The Sex Binary Is Not a 'Western Construct,' Gender Identity Is," *Feminist Current*, December 6, 2020, https://www.feministcurrent.com/2020/12/06/the-sex-binary-is-not-a-western-construct-gender-identity-is/.

27. Amrou Al-Kadhi, "How Britain's Colonial Past Can Be Traced Through to the Transphobic Feminism of Today," *Independent*, June 10, 2020, https://www.independent.co.uk/voices/transphobia-sex-gender-white-supremacy-racism-jk-rowling-a9557996.html.

28. Beatrice, "Sex Binary."

29. Beatrice, "Sex Binary."

30. Serena Nanda, *Neither Man nor Woman: The Hijras of India* (Belmont, CA: Wadsworth, 1990).

31. Renate Syed, "Hijras: India's Third Gender and 2500 Years of Discrimination and Exclusion," handout presented at "Gender and Violence," Indo-German International Conference, Jawaharlal Nehru University, September 22–24, 2015, https://www.renate-syed.de/artikel/renate

-syed-hijras-india-s-third-gender-and-2500-years-of-discrimination
-and-exclusion.

32. Syed, "Hijras."

33. Frank Krishner, "Transgender vs. Hijra Debate Hots Up," *Times of India*, February 9, 2015, https://timesofindia.indiatimes.com/city/patna/transgender-vs-hijra-debate-hots-up/articleshow/46169219.cms?from=mdr.

34. On the Kathoey, see Peter A. Jackson, *Dear Uncle Go: Male Homosexuality in Thailand* (Bangkok: Bua Luang Books, 1995).

35. Marie-Thérèse Claes, "Kathoeys of Thailand: A Diversity Case in International Business," *International Journal of Diversity in Organisations, Communities, and Nations* 10, no. 5 (2011): 183–97, quote from 188.

36. Claes, "Kathoeys," 190.

37. Claes, "Kathoeys," 188.

38. Beatrice, "Sex Binary."

39. Beatrice, "Sex Binary."

40. Beatrice, "Sex Binary."

41. Deirdre Bell, "Toward an End to Appropriation of Indigenous 'Two-Spirit' People in Trans Politics: The Relationship Between Third Gender Roles and Patriarchy," *Culturally Bound Gender*, March 9, 2013, https://culturallyboundgender.wordpress.com/2013/03/09/toward-an-end-to-appropriation-of-indigenous-two-spirit-people-in-trans-politics-the-relationship-between-third-gender-roles-and-patriarchy/.

42. Bell, "End to Appropriation."

43. Andrew Higgins, "With More Freedom, Young Women in Albania Shun Tradition of 'Sworn Virgins,'" *New York Times*, August 8, 2021, https://www.nytimes.com/2021/08/08/world/europe/sworn-virgins-albania.html.

44. Tui McLean, "The Last of Albania's 'Sworn Virgins,'" BBC News, December 10, 2022, https://www.bbc.com/news/world-europe-63904744.

45. McLean, "Last of Albania's"; Higgins, "More Freedom."

46. Higgins, "More Freedom."

47. Higgins, "More Freedom."

48. Higgins, "More Freedom."

49. Higgins, "More Freedom."

50. Higgins, "More Freedom."

51. Higgins, "More Freedom."

52. Higgins, "More Freedom."

53. McLean, "Last of Albania's"

54. McLean, "Last of Albania's"

55. "The Third Gender and Hijras: Hinduism Case Study—Gender," Harvard Divinity School, 2018, https://rpl.hds.harvard.edu/religion -context/case-studies/gender/third-gender-and-hijras.

56. Dorothy Ko, *Cinderella's Sisters: A Revisionist History of Footbinding* (Berkeley: University of California Press, 2005), 261, note 3. According to Ko, "modern analyses of material cultures and gender perceptions do suggest that footbinding as a social practice was likely to have begun in the tenth century."

57. Wang Ping, *Aching for Beauty* (New York: Knopf Doubleday, 2002), 6.

58. Wang, *Aching*, 4–5.

59. Ko, *Cinderella's Sisters*, 2.

60. Wang, *Aching*, 34.

61. Wang, *Aching*, 33.

62. Wang, *Aching*, 32.

63. Wang, *Aching*, 19

64. Ko, *Cinderella's Sisters*, 1–2.

65. Ko, *Cinderella's Sisters*, 102.

66. Ko, *Cinderella's Sisters*, 1.

67. George C. Denniston and Marilyn Fayre Milos, eds., *Sexual Mutilations: A Human Tragedy* (Boston: Springer, 1997), https://link.springer .com/book/10.1007/978-1-4757-2679-4.

68. Didier Diers and Xavier Valla, "The Skoptzy," in *Sexual Mutilations*, ed. George C. Denniston and Marilyn Fayre Milos (Boston: Springer, 1997), 63–66, https://doi.org/10.1007/978-1-4757-2679-4_4.

69. Wang, *Aching*, 33.

70. Wang, *Aching*, 36–37.

71. See Ko, *Cinderella's Sisters*, 14ff.

72. Introductory note to "Women Have Gone to the Labour Front" (1955), in *The Socialist Upsurge in China's Countryside*, Chinese ed., vol. 1, quoted in chap. 31, *Quotations from Mao Tse Tung* (1966), accessed March 6, 2024, https://www.marxists.org/reference/archive/mao /works/red-book/ch31.htm.

73. Fu Wen, "Doctrine of Confucius and Mencius—the Shackle That Keeps Women in Bondage," *Peking Review*, no. 10 (March 8, 1974):

16–18, https://www.marxists.org/subject/china/peking-review/1974 /PR1974-10c.htm, accessed March 6, 2024

74. The "three obediences" (*san cong* 三從) are discussed in the introduction above. The "four virtues (*si de* 四德) are mentioned in various Confucian texts, especially on ritual and moral conduct. A short overview with reference to source texts is found here: "Three Obediences and Four Virtues," Wikipedia, accessed March 11, 2025, https://en.wikipedia .org/wiki/Three_Obediences_and_Four_Virtues.

75. Fu, "Doctrine of Confucius and Mencius."

76. Introductory note to "Solving the Labour Shortage by Arousing the Women to Join in Production" (1955), in *The Socialist Upsurge in China's Countryside*, Chinese ed., vol. 2, quoted in *Quotations from Mao Tse Tung*, chap. 31, accessed March 6, 2024, https://www.marxists.org /reference/archive/mao/works/red-book/ch31.htm.

77. Soong Ching Ling, "Women's Liberation in China," *Peking Review*, no. 6 (February 11, 1972): 6–7, https://www.marxists.org/subject/china /peking-review/1972/PR1972-06a.htm.

78. Soong, "Women's Liberation."

79. See, e.g., "Freedom Cannot Be Given: An Analysis of the Significance of Women in the Cultural Revolution," by Zhen Tian, *The UC Santa Barbara Undergraduate Journal of History* (Fall 2021), https://under gradjournal.history.ucsb.edu/our-journal/past-issues/fall-2021/tian/.

4. TRANSGENDER AND
THE AUTHENTICITY NARRATIVE

1. Azeen Ghorayshi, "Report Reveals Sharp Rise in Transgender Young People in the U.S.," *New York Times*, June 10, 2022, https://www .nytimes.com/2022/06/10/science/transgender-teenagers-national -survey.html.

2. Walter Bouman, Wim Van den Noortgate, Laurence Claes, Gemma Witcomb, and Fernando Fernandez-Aranda, "Systematic Review and Meta-Analysis of Prevalence Studies in Transsexualism," *European Psychiatry* 30 (2015): 10.1016/j.eurpsy.2015.04.005.

3. Kacie M. Kidd et al. "Prevalence of Gender-Diverse Youth in an Urban School District," *Pediatrics* 147, no. 6 (2021), https://doi.org/10.1542/peds .2020-049823.

4. Pablo Expósito-Campos et al., "Gender Detransition: A Critical Review of the Literature," *Actas Españolas de Psiquiatría* 51, no. 3 (2023): 98–118.

5. Maria Loos, Sabine Hannema, Daniel Klink, Martin den Heijer, and Chantal Wiepjes, "Continuation of Gender-Affirming Hormones in Transgender People Starting Puberty Suppression in Adolescence: A Cohort Study in the Netherlands," *Lancet Child & Adolescent Health* 6 (2022): 10.1016/S2352-4642(22)00254-1.

6. Mobeen Azhar, "Pakistan's Traditional Third Gender Isn't Happy with the Trans Movement," *The World*, July 27, 2017. https://theworld .org/stories/2017/07/27/pakistans-traditional-third-gender-isnt-happy -trans-movement.

7. Azhar, "Pakistan's Traditional Third Gender."

8. Azhar, "Pakistan's Traditional Third Gender."

9. "List of Gender Identities," Wikipedia, accessed March 11, 2025, https://en.wikipedia.org/wiki/List_of_gender_identities.

10. Natalie Wynn, "Twilight," *ContraPoints*, March 2, 2024, YouTube, 2:25:26, https://www.youtube.com/watch?v=bqloPw5wp48.

11. Natalie Wynn, "Pronouns," *ContraPoints*, November 3, 2018, YouTube, 31:55, ca. 27:02, https://www.youtube.com/watch?v=9bbINLWtMKI &t=1622s.

12. Natalie Wynn, "Pronouns," ca. 28:11, https://www.youtube.com/watch ?v=9bbINLWtMKI&t=1691s.

13. Natalie Wynn, "J. K. Rowling," *ContraPoints*, January 26, 2021, You-Tube, 1:29:44, ca. 28:11, https://www.youtube.com/watch?v=7gDKbT _l2us&t=1691s.

14. Natalie Wynn, "Gender Critical," *ContraPoints*, March 31, 2019, You-Tube, 33:48, ca. 8:20, https://www.youtube.com/watch?v=1pTPuoGj QsI&t=500s.

15. Wynn, "Rowling," ca. 31:31, https://www.youtube.com/watch?v =7gDKbT_l2us&t=1891s.

16. Natalie Wynn, "Autogynephilia," *ContraPoints*, February 2, 2018, You-Tube, 48:54, ca. 15:14, https://www.youtube.com/watch?v=6czRFLs5 JQo&t=914s.

17. Wynn, "Autogynephilia," ca. 14:34, https://www.youtube.com/watch ?v=6czRFLs5JQo&t=874s.

18. Wynn, "Rowling," ca. 9:31, https://www.youtube.com/watch?v =7gDKbT_l2us&t=571s.

19. Wynn, "Gender Critical," ca. 10:26, https://www.youtube.com/watch?v=1pTPuoGjQsI&t=626s.

20. Judith Butler, *Gender Trouble* (London: Routledge, 1990).

21. Natalie Wynn, "Transtrenders," *ContraPoints*, July 2, 2019, YouTube, 34:43, https://www.youtube.com/watch?v=EdvM_pRfuFM&t=1480s. Here, while generally embracing it, Wynn objects to Butler's concept as being both too inclusive (because it would also apply to people simply playing a gender) and too exclusive of people who identify with a gender without being able to perform it convincingly.

22. Wynn, "Pronouns," ca. 22:58, https://www.youtube.com/watch?v=9bbINLWtMKI&t=1378s.

23. Wynn, "Pronouns," ca. 22:58, https://www.youtube.com/watch?v=9bbINLWtMKI&t=1378s.

24. Wynn, "Rowling," ca. 1:23:16, https://www.youtube.com/watch?v=7gDKbT_l2us&t=4996s.

25. Wynn, "Autogynephilia," ca. 22:24, https://www.youtube.com/watch?v=6czRFLs5JQo&t=1344s.

26. Wynn, "Autogynephilia," ca. 46:00, https://www.youtube.com/watch?v=6czRFLs5JQo&t=2760s.

27. Wynn, "Gender Critical," ca. 33:49, https://www.youtube.com/watch?v=1pTPuoGjQsI&t=540s.

28. Wynn, ca. "Gender Critical," ca. 9:26, https://www.youtube.com/watch?v=1pTPuoGjQsI&t=566s.

29. Wynn, "Gender Critical," ca. 9:36, https://www.youtube.com/watch?v=1pTPuoGjQsI&t=576s.

30. Wynn, "Twilight," ca. 2:40:07, https://www.youtube.com/watch?v=bqloPw5wp48&t=9607s.

31. Marshall McLuhan and Quentin Fiore, *The Medium Is the Massage* (London: Penguin, 1967), 77.

32. McLuhan and Fiore, *Medium*, 77.

33. Stacey Hurley, "Ask Stacey: How Do I Support My Friend Aho Who Is Transgender?," *Dundalk Eagle*, December 21, 2021, https://www.dundalkeagle.com/opinion/ask-stacy-how-do-i-support-my-friend-who-is-transgender/article_df230749-4212-53d5-9c68-d965e6cc798d.html.

34. Jamie Zapata, "Transgender Day of Remembrance Is a Time for Authenticity," *Inman*, November 18, 2023, https://www.inman.com

/2023/11/18/transgender-day-of-remembrance-is-a-time-for-auth
enticity/.

35. Amazon page for *Authentic Selves: Celebrating Trans and Nonbinary
People and Their Families*, ed. Peggy Gillespie, https://www.amazon
.com/Authentic-Selves-Celebrating-Nonbinary-Families/dp
/1558968962.

36. "Always Jane," Wikipedia, accessed March 11, 2025, https://en
.wikipedia.org/wiki/Always_Jane.

37. "Always Jane," Wikipedia.

38. Always Jane, TVBD, accessed March 11, 2025, https://thetvdb.com
/series/always-jane.

39. Adrian Horton, "'It's Not Just About Being Trans:' Always Jane Is a
Moving, Intimate Portrait of Late Adolescence," *The Guardian*,
November 9, 2021, https://www.theguardian.com/tv-and-radio/2021
/nov/09/always-jane-amazon-transgender-coming-of-age.

40. Kristen Lopez, "'Always Jane' Review: Trans Docuseries Is a Sweet
Yet Far Too Simple Exploration of Finding Oneself," *IndieWire*,
November 12, 2021, https://www.indiewire.com/features/general
/always-jane-review-trans-docuseries-1234678499/.

41. Jen Christensen, "Gender-Affirming Surgeries in the U.S. Nearly Tripled from 2016 to 2019, Study Finds," CNN, August 23, 2023, https://
edition.cnn.com/2023/08/23/health/gender-affirming-surgery-study
/index.html.

42. Grand View Research, *U.S. Sex Reassignment Surgery Market Size,
Share & Trends Analysis Report by Gender Transition (Female-to-Male,
Male-to-Female), by Procedure (Mastectomy, Vaginoplasty, Scrotoplasty,
Hysterectomy, Phalloplasty), and Segment Forecasts, 2023–2030* (San Fran-
cisco: Grand View Research, 2023), https://www.grandviewresearch
.com/industry-analysis/us-sex-reassignment-surgery-market.

43. "About ART Surgical," ART Surgical, accessed March 1, 2025, https://
www.artsurgical.net/about-art-surgical.

44. "Gender and Sexual Health Services," Brown University Health,
accessed March 11, 2025, https://www.brownhealth.org/centers-ser
vices/gender-and-sexual-health-services.

45. Brooke Sopelsa, "NYC Launches Ad Campaign Affirming Trans
Bathroom Rights," NBC News, June 7, 2016, https://www.nbcnews

.com/feature/nbc-out/nyc-launches-ad-campaign-affirming-trans
-bathroom-rights-n586726.

46. "Coming Out: Living Authentically as Transgender or Non-Binary,"
Human Rights Campaign Foundation, updated October 2022, https://
reports.hrc.org/coming-out-living-authentically-as-transgender-non
-binary?.

47. Jo Yurcaba, "'Social Contagion' Isn't Causing More Youths to Be
Transgender, Study Finds," NBC News, August 4, 2022, https://www
.nbcnews.com/nbc-out/out-health-and-wellness/social-contagion
-isnt-causing-youths-transgender-study-finds-rcna41392.

48. Lisa Littman, "Parent Reports of Adolescents and Young Adults Perceived to Show Signs of a Rapid Onset of Gender Dysphoria," *PLoS
ONE* 13, no. 8 (2018), https://doi.org/10.1371/journal.pone.0202330;
K. C. Pang et al., "Association of Media Coverage of Transgender and
Gender Diverse Issues with Rates of Referral of Transgender Children
and Adolescents to Specialist Gender Clinics in the UK and Australia," *JAMA Network Open* 3, no. 7 (2020), https://doi.org/10.1001
/jamanetworkopen.2020.11161.

49. "Rapid-onset gender dysphoria controversy," Wikipedia, accessed
March 11, 2025, https://en.wikipedia.org/wiki/Rapid-onset_gender
_dysphoria_controversy#cite_note-hrc-35.

50. Ghorayshi, "Sharp Rise."

51. Leonie Crosse, "Respecting the Free Will, Authenticity, and Autonomy of Transgender Youth," *Nursing Ethics* (2023), https://doi.org/10
.1177/09697330231180743.

52. Leonie Crosse, LinkedIn, accessed March 11, 2025, https://au.linkedin
.com/in/leonie-crosse-6bbb24242.

53. Robert Sapolsky, *Determined: A Science of Life Without Free Will*
(Penguin, 2023).

54. Bundesamt für Justiz, *Gesetz über die Selbstbestimmung in Bezug auf den
Geschlechtseintrag (SBGG)* (Law on the self-determination with regard
to the gender entry), June 19, 2024, https://www.gesetze-im-internet
.de/sbgg/SBGG.pdf.

55. Deutscher Bundestag, *Gesetzentwurf der Bundesregierung: Entwurf
eines Gesetzes über die Selbstbestimmung in Bezug auf den Geschlechtseintrag und zur Änderung weiterer Vorschriften* (Federal government bill:

Draft of a law on the self-determination with regard to the gender entry and on the modification of further regulations), Drucksache 20/9049, November 1, 2023, https://dserver.bundestag.de/btd/20/090/2009049 .pdf. The bill for the law that was approved by the German parliament on June 19, 2024, is an extensive document outlining in detail its rationale and legal context; SBGG, 22.

56. Deutscher Bundestag, "Gesetzentwurf zur Änderung des Geschlechtseintrags debattiert," November 20, 2023, YouTube, 1:06:40, https://www.youtube.com/watch?v=PkgjqfIpnWo

57. Deutscher Bundestag, "Gesetzentwurf der Bundesregierung," 1.

58. Deutscher Bundestag, "Gesetzentwurf der Bundesregierung," 19.

59. Deutscher Bundestag, "Gesetzentwurf der Bundesregierung," 25.

60. Charles Taylor, *The Ethics of Authenticity* (Cambridge, MA: Harvard University Press, 1992), 74.

61. Deutscher Bundestag, "Gesetzentwurf der Bundesregierung," 25.

62. Deutscher Bundestag, "Gesetzentwurf der Bundesregierung," 22.

63. Taylor, *Ethics*, 74.

64. Deutscher Bundestag, "Gesetzentwurf der Bundesregierung," 25.

65. Deutscher Bundestag, "Gesetzentwurf der Bundesregierung," 19.

66. Deutscher Bundestag, "Gesetzentwurf der Bundesregierung," 41.

67. See, e.g., Mine Pleasure Bouvar, "Selbstbetrug statt Selbstbestimmung: Queere Verbände verkaufen die geplante Reform der rechtlichen Anerkennung für trans und inter Personen als Fortschritt—was sie nicht ist," *analyse & kritik*, June 20, 2023, https://www.akweb.de /politik/selbstbestimmungsgesetz-sbgg-tsg-trans-inter-personen -kritik/.

68. See, e.g., "Trans-Gesetz: Wissen sie, was sie tun?," *Emma*, October 25, 2023, https://www.emma.de/artikel/wissen-sie-was-sie-tun-340653.

69. Jean-Paul Sartre, *No Exit and Three Other Plays*, trans. Stuart Gilbert (New York: Vintage, 1989).

70. Jean-Paul Sartre, Michel Contat, and Michel Rybalka, *Sartre on Theater* (London: Random House, 1976), 199; Domi Gulminelli, "Sartre— L'enfer, c'est les autres 'Explications,'" March 21, 2016, YouTube, 5:54, https://www.youtube.com/watch?v=Q6-RWlmtqkY&t=4s.

71. Sartre, *Sartre on Theater*, 43.

72. Sartre, *Sartre on Theater*, 199–200.

73. Simone de Beauvoir, *The Second Sex* (*Le Deuxième Sexe*, 1949), trans. by H. M. Parshley (New York: Penguin, 1972), 267.

74. "To begin with, there will always be certain differences between man and woman; her eroticism, and therefore her sexual world, have a special form of their own and therefore cannot fail to engender a sensuality, a sensitivity, of a special nature. . . . As a matter of fact, man, like woman, is flesh, therefore passive, the plaything of his hormones and of the species, the restless prey of his desires. And she, like him, in the midst of the carnal fever, is a consenting, a voluntary gift, an activity; they live out in their several fashions the strange ambiguity of existence made body." Beauvoir, *Second Sex*, 683.

75. Beauvoir, *Second Sex*, 14. I was unable to find the source of the quote in Parker's writings. Perhaps Beauvoir was quoting from memory or hearsay.

76. Beauvoir, *Second Sex*, 14.

77. Beauvoir, *Second Sex*, 686.

78. Karl Marx, *The German Ideology* (1845), part 1, "Feuerbach: Opposition of the Materialist and Idealist Outlook," https://www.marxists .org/archive/marx/works/1845/german-ideology/ch01.htm.

79. Marx, *German Ideology*.

80. Beauvoir, *Second Sex*, 681.

81. On the definition of a simulacrum as a copy without an original, see Jean Baudrillard, *Simulacres et Simulation* (Paris: Éditions Galilée, 1981).

82. An extended version of the following analysis of feminine-gender profiling in Queens has been published in collaboration with Jorge Ponseti, Paul D'Ambrosio, and Aglaja Stirn: "Transformation: From (Trans-)Gender Roles to Profiles," *Linacre Quarterly* 91, no. 3 (2023): 278–95.

83. Rotten Tomatoes, "Season 1—Queens," 2021, accessed March 1, 2025, https://www.rottentomatoes.com/tv/queens/s01.

84. "*Queens* (American TV series)," Wikipedia, accessed March 11, 2025, https://en.wikipedia.org/wiki/Queens_(American_TV_series)#cite _note-32.

85. *Queens*, "Nasty Girl," October 1, 2021, YouTube, 3:35, accessed March 1, 2024, https://www.youtube.com/watch?v=H605IhaMdzM&list =RDH605IhaMdzM&start_radio=1.

86. " 'Nasty Girl' lyrics," AZLyrics, accessed March 16, 2025, https://www
.azlyrics.com/lyrics/eve/nastygirl.html.

87. Beauvoir, *Second Sex*, 677.

88. Julia Anton, "Ranking deutscher Influencer: Reich dank Reichweite,"
Frankfurter Allgemeine, December 14, 2021, https://www.faz.net/aktuell
/stil/trends-nischen/das-sind-die-wertvollsten-deutschen-influencer
-ganz-vorne-nur-frauen-17684153.html; Batten & Company, "Brands
im Ringlicht: Das sind Deutschlands wertvollste Influencer:innen,"
November 29, 2021, https://www.batten-company.com/news/brands
-im-ringlicht-das-sind-deutschlands-wertvollste-influencerinnen
studie-zum-markenwert-von-deutschlands-erfolgreichsten-influ
encerinnen/. Translations from the FAZ report are mine.

89. Wynn, "Twilight," ca. 2:40:07, https://www.youtube.com/watch?v
=bqloPw5wp48&t=9607s.

90. Wynn, "Twilight," ca. 9:26, https://www.youtube.com/watch?v
=bqloPw5wp48&t=566s.

CONCLUSION

1. Hans-Georg Moeller and Paul J. D'Ambrosio, *You and Your Profile:
Identity After Authenticity* (New York: Columbia University Press,
2021).

2. Jared Morningstar, "Trans and Nonbinary Identity in the Age of Profilicity," Medium, October 29, 2021, https://jaredmorningstar.medium
.com/trans-and-nonbinary-identity-in-the-age-of-profilicity-65f6162
d823c.

3. Thorsten Botz-Bornstein, "Zhuangzi, Language & Gender," *Philosophy
Now*, 2022, https://philosophynow.org/issues/150/Zhuangzi_Language
_and_Gender.

4. Botz-Bornstein, "Zhuangzi, Language & Gender."

5. Botz-Bornstein, "Zhuangzi, Language & Gender."

6. Morningstar, "Trans and Nonbinary Identity."

BIBLIOGRAPHY

Al-Kadhi, Amrou. "How Britain's Colonial Past Can Be Traced Through to the Transphobic Feminism of Today." *Independent*, June 10, 2020. https://www.independent.co.uk/voices/transphobia-sex-gender-white-supremacy-racism-jk-rowling-a9557996.html.

"Always Jane." TVBD. https://thetvdb.com/series/always-jane.

Anderson, E. N. "Flowering Apricot: Environmental Practice, Folk Religion, and Daoism." In *Daoism and Ecology: Ways Within a Cosmic Landscape*, edited by N. J. Girardot et al. Cambridge, MA: Harvard University Press, 2001.

Anton, Julia. "Ranking deutscher Influencer: Reich dank Reichweite." *Frankfurter Allgemeine*, December 14, 2021. https://www.faz.net/aktuell/stil/trends-nischen/das-sind-die-wertvollsten-deutschen-influencer-ganz-vorne-nur-frauen-17684153.html.

ART Surgical. "About ART Surgical." https://www.artsurgical.net/about-art-surgical.

"Authentic Selves: Celebrating Trans and Nonbinary People and Their Families, [edited] by Peggy Gillespie." Amazon. https://www.amazon.com/Authentic-Selves-Celebrating-Nonbinary-Families/dp/1558968962.

Azhar, Mobeen. "Pakistan's Traditional Third Gender Isn't Happy with the Trans Movement." *The World*, July 27, 2017. https://theworld.org/stories/2017/07/27/pakistans-traditional-third-gender-isnt-happy-trans-movement.

Baldrian-Hussein, Farzeen. "Hun and Po 魂·魄: Yang Soul(s) and Yin Soul(s); Celestial Soul(s) and Earthly Soul(s)." In *The Encyclopedia of Taoism*, edited by Fabrizio Pregadio, 521–23. London: Routledge, 2008.

Batten & Company. "Brands im Ringlicht: Das sind Deutschlands wertvollste Influencer:innen." November 29, 2021. https://www.batten -company.com/news/brands-im-ringlicht-das-sind-deutschlands -wertvollste-influencerinnenstudie-zum-markenwert-von-deutschlands -erfolgreichsten-influencerinnen/.

Baudrillard, Jean. *Simulacres et Simulation*. Paris: Éditions Galilée, 1981.

Beatrice, L. "The Sex Binary Is Not a 'Western Construct,' Gender Identity is." *Feminist Current*, December 6, 2020. https://www.feministcurrent .com/2020/12/06/the-sex-binary-is-not-a-western-construct-gender -identity-is/.

Beauvoir, Simone de. *The Second Sex*. Translated by H. M. Parshley. New York: Penguin, 1972 (1949).

Bell, Deirdre. "Toward an End to Appropriation of Indigenous 'Two-Spirit' People in Trans Politics: The Relationship Between Third Gender Roles and Patriarchy." *Culturally Bound Gender*, March 9, 2013. https:// culturallyboundgender.wordpress.com/2013/03/09/toward-an-end-to -appropriation-of-indigenous-two-spirit-people-in-trans-politics-the -relationship-between-third-gender-roles-and-patriarchy/.

Botz-Bornstein, Thorsten. "Zhuangzi, Language & Gender." *Philosophy Now* 150 (June–July 2022). https://philosophynow.org/issues/150/Zhuangzi _Language_and_Gender.

Bouman, Walter, Wim Van den Noortgate, Laurence Claes, Gemma Witcomb, and Fernando Fernandez-Aranda. "Systematic Review and Meta-Analysis of Prevalence Studies in Transsexualism." *European Psychiatry* 30 (2015): https://doi.org/10.1016/j.eurpsy.2015.04.005.

Bouvar, Mine Pleasure. "Selbstbetrug statt Selbstbestimmung: Queere Verbände verkaufen die geplante Reform der rechtlichen Anerkennung für trans und inter Personen als Fortschritt—was sie nicht ist," *analyse & kritik*, June 20, 2023. https://www.akweb.de/politik/selbstbestimmungs gesetz-sbgg-tsg-trans-inter-personen-kritik/.

Brown University Health. "Gender and Sexual Health Services." https:// www.brownhealth.org/centers-services/gender-and-sexual-health -services

Buber, Martin. *Reden und Gleichnisse des Tschuang-Tse*. Leipzig: Insel, 1921.

Bundesamt für Justiz. *Gesetz über die Selbstbestimmung in Bezug auf den Geschlechtseintrag (SBGG)* (Law on the self-determination with regard to the gender entry). https://www.gesetze-im-internet.de/sbgg/SBGG.pdf.

Butler, Judith. *Gender Trouble*. London: Routledge. 1990.

Cabe, Benjamin. "On Gender and the Soul." *Theoria: Orthodox Christian Faith and Culture*, October 29, 2022. https://theoriatv.substack.com/p/on -gender-and-the-soul.

"China Fertility Rate (1950–2025)." Macrotrends. https://www.macrotrends .net/global-metrics/countries/CHN/china/fertility-rate.

Chinese Text Project. https://ctext.org/.

Christensen, Jen. "Gender-Affirming Surgeries in the U.S. Nearly Tripled from 2016 to 2019, Study Finds." CNN, August 23, 2023. https://edition .cnn.com/2023/08/23/health/gender-affirming-surgery-study/index .html.

Claes, Marie-Thérèse. "Kathoeys of Thailand: A Diversity Case in International Business." *International Journal of Diversity in Organisations, Communities, and Nations* 10, no. 5 (2011): 183–97.

Crosse, Leonie. "Respecting the Free Will, Authenticity, and Autonomy of Transgender Youth." Nursing Ethics 31, nos. 2–3 (2023). https://doi.org /10.1177/09697330231180743.

Cyril of Jerusalem. "Catechetical Lecture 4: On the Ten Points of Doctrine." *New Advent*. Accessed March 10, 2025. https://www.newadvent.org /fathers/310104.htm.

D'Ambrosio, Paul, Hans-Rudolf Kantor, and Hans-Georg Moeller. "Incongruent Names: A Theme in the History of Chinese Philosophy." *Dao: A Journal of Comparative Philosophy* 17, no. 3 (2018).

Denniston, George C., and Marilyn Fayre Milos, eds. *Sexual Mutilations: A Human Tragedy*. New York: Springer, 1997. https://link.springer.com /book/10.1007/978-1-4757-2679-4.

Deutscher Bundestag. *Gesetzentwurf der Bundesregierung: Entwurf eines Gesetzes über die Selbstbestimmung in Bezug auf den Geschlechtseintrag und zur Änderung weiterer Vorschriften* (Federal government bill: Draft of a law on the self-determination with regard to the gender entry and on the modification of further regulations). Drucksache 20/9049, November 1, 2023. https://dserver.bundestag.de/btd/20/090/2009049.pdf.

——. "Gesetzentwurf zur Änderung des Geschlechtseintrags debattiert." November 20, 2023. YouTube, 1:06:40. https://www.youtube.com/watch?v=PkgjqfIpnWo.

Diers, Didier, and Xavier Valla. "The Skoptzy." In *Sexual Mutilations*, edited by George C. Denniston and Marilyn Fayre Milos, 63–66. Boston: Springer, 1997. https://doi.org/10.1007/978-1-4757-2679-4_4.

Dommaraju, Premchand, and Gavin Jones. "Divorce Trends in Asia." *Asian Journal of Social Science* 39, no. 6 (2011): 725–50. https://doi.org/10.1163/156853111X619201.

Dover, Kenneth J. *Greek Homosexuality*. Cambridge, MA: Harvard University Press, 1978.

"Eastern Philosophy—Lao Tzu." *The School of Life*. November 21, 2014. YouTube, 10:02. https://www.youtube.com/watch?v=dFb7Hxva5rg.

Eccles, John. *Evolution of the Brain: Creation of the Self*. New York: Routledge, 1989.

——. *How the Self Controls Its Brain*. New York: Springer-Verlag, 1994.

Esposito, Elena. *Kommunikation mit unverständlichen Maschinen*. Vienna: Residenz Verlag, 2024.

Expósito-Campos, Pablo, Rubén Gómez-Gil, Beatriz Fernández-Rivas, Francisca Villada-Plasco, Sergio Castillón-Sánchez, and Antonio González-Rodríguez. "Gender Detransition: A Critical Review of the Literature." *Actas Españolas de Psiquiatría* 51, no. 3 (2023): 98–118.

Feuchtwang, Stephan. "Chinese Religions." In *Religions in the Modern World: Traditions and Transformations*, edited by Linda Woodhead, Christopher Partridge, and Hiroko Kawanami, 143–72. New York: Routledge, 2016.

Fu Wen. "Doctrine of Confucius and Mencius—the Shackle That Keeps Women in Bondage." *Peking Review*, no. 10 (March 8, 1974): 16–18. Accessed March 6, 2024. https://www.marxists.org/subject/china/peking-review/1974/PR1974-10c.htm.

Fukuyama, Francis. *The End of History and the Last Man*. New York: Free Press, 1992.

Ghorayshi, Azeen. "Report Reveals Sharp Rise in Transgender Young People in the U.S." *New York Times*, June 10, 2022. https://www.nytimes.com/2022/06/10/science/transgender-teenagers-national-survey.html.

Giles, Herbert A. *Chuang Tzu: Mystic, Moralist, and Social Reformer*. London: Bernard Quaritch, 1889. https://www.gutenberg.org/files/59709/59709-h/59709-h.htm.

Glocker, Melanie L., Daniel D. Langleben, Kosha Ruparel, James W. Loughead, Ruben C. Gur, and Norbert Sachser. "Baby Schema in Infant Faces Induces Cuteness Perception and Motivation for Caretaking in Adults." *Ethology* 115, no. 3 (2009): 257–63. https://doi.org/10.1111/j.1439 -0310.2008.01603.x.

Graham, A. C. *Chuang Tzu: The Inner Chapters.* Indianapolis: Hackett, 2001.

Grand View Research. *U.S. Sex Reassignment Surgery Market Size, Share & Trends Analysis Report by Gender Transition (Female-to-Male, Male-to-Female), by Procedure (Mastectomy, Vaginoplasty, Scrotoplasty, Hysterectomy, Phalloplasty), and Segment Forecasts, 2023–2030.* San Francisco: Grand View Research: 2023. https://www.grandviewresearch.com/industry -analysis/us-sex-reassignment-surgery-market.

Hanfeizi. *Han Feizi: Basic Writings.* Translated by Burton Watson. New York: Columbia University Press, 1964.

Harvard Divinity School. "The Third Gender and Hijras: Hinduism Case Study—Gender." https://rpl.hds.harvard.edu/religion-context/case -studies/gender/third-gender-and-hijras. 2018.

Hebblethwaite, Brian. *Philosophical Theology and Christian Doctrine.* Wiley Blackwell, 2005.

Higgins, Andrew. "With More Freedom, Young Women in Albania Shun Tradition of 'Sworn Virgins.'" *New York Times*, August 8, 2021. https:// www.nytimes.com/2021/08/08/world/europe/sworn-virgins-albania .html.

Hofstede, Geert. *Culture's Consequences: Comparing Values, Behaviors, Insti- tutions, and Organizations Across Nations.* 2nd ed. Thousand Oaks, CA: Sage, 2001.

Hoon Chang Yau. "Revisiting the Asian Values Argument Used by Asian Political Leaders and Its Validity." *Indonesian Quarterly* 32, no. 2 (2004): 154–74.

Horton, Adrian. "'It's Not Just About Being Trans': Always Jane Is a Mov- ing, Intimate Portrait of Late Adolescence." *The Guardian*, November 9, 2021. https://www.theguardian.com/tv-and-radio/2021/nov/09/always -jane-amazon-transgender-coming-of-age.

Hosanagar, Kartik. *A Human's Guide to Machine Intelligence: How Algorithms Are Shaping Our Lives and How We Can Stay in Control.* New York: Viking, 2019.

Human Rights Campaign Foundation. "Coming Out: Living Authentically as Transgender or Non-Binary." https://reports.hrc.org/coming-out -living-authentically-as-transgender-non-binary?

Hurley, Stacey. "Ask Stacey: How Do I Support My Friend Aho Who Is Transgender?" *The Dundalk Eagle*, December 21, 2021. https://www .dundalkeagle.com/opinion/ask-stacy-how-do-i-support-my-friend-who -is-transgender/article_df230749-4212-53d5-9c68-d965e6cc798d.html.

Jackson, Peter A. *Dear Uncle Go: Male Homosexuality in Thailand*. Bangkok: Bua Luang Books, 1995.

Kant, Immanuel. "An Answer to the Question: What Is Enlightenment?" Translated by Ted Humphrey. Hackett, 1992. https://www.nypl.org/sites /default/files/kant_whatisenlightenment.pdf.

——. *Kritik der reinen Vernunft*. Hamburg, Germany: Felix Meiner Verlag, 1988.

Kaufman, Scott Barry. "Taking Sex Differences in Personality Seriously." *Scientific American*, December 12, 2019. Accessed March 20, 2024. https:// www.scientificamerican.com/blog/beautiful-minds/taking-sex -differences-in-personality-seriously/.

Kidd, Kacie M., Greta R. Bauer, Johanna Bohlen, Maeve Tharp, and Robert Garofalo. "Prevalence of Gender-Diverse Youth in an Urban School District." *Pediatrics* 147, no. 6 (2021): https://doi.org/10.1542/peds.2020-049823.

Ko, Dorothy. *Cinderella's Sisters: A Revisionist History of Footbinding*. Berkeley: University of California Press, 2005.

Konstantinovskaia, Natalia. "Being Kawaii in Japan." UCLA Center for the Study of Women, July 21, 2017. https://csw.ucla.edu/2017/07/21/being -kawaii-in-japan/.

Krishner, Frank. "Transgender vs. Hijra Debate Hots Up." *Times of India*, February 9, 2015. https://timesofindia.indiatimes.com/city/patna /transgender-vs-hijra-debate-hots-up/articleshow/46169219.cms?from =mdr.

Kwan, Michael. "What Killed Marriage? China's Divorce Rate Is up 75% in a Decade." China Europe International Business School, December 2, 2021. https://www.ceibs.edu/new-papers-columns/20503.

Lau, Dim C., trans. *Mencius: Translated, with an Introduction by D. C. Lau*. London: Penguin, 1970.

Lear, Andrew, and Eva Cantarella. *Images of Ancient Greek Pederasty: Boys Were Their Gods*. London: Routledge, 2009.

Legge, James. *The Sacred Books of China: The Texts of Taoism*. Oxford: Clarendon Press, 1891. https://ctext.org/dictionary.pl?if=en&id=2732.

Littlejohn, Ronnie. "Daoist Philosophy." *Internet Encyclopedia of Philosophy*. https://iep.utm.edu/daoism-daoist-philosophy/.

Littman, Lisa. "Parent Reports of Adolescents and Young Adults Perceived to Show Signs of a Rapid Onset of Gender Dysphoria." *PLoS ONE* 13, no. 8 (2018): https://doi.org/10.1371/journal.pone.0202330.

Loos, Maria, Sabine Hannema, Daniel Klink, Martin den Heijer, and Chantal Wiepjes. "Continuation of Gender-Affirming Hormones in Transgender People Starting Puberty Suppression in Adolescence: A Cohort Study in the Netherlands." *The Lancet Child & Adolescent Health* 6 (2022): https://doi.org/10.1016/S2352-4642(22)00254-1.

Lopez, Kristen. "'Always Jane' Review: Trans Docuseries Is a Sweet Yet Far Too Simple Exploration of Finding Oneself." *IndieWire*, November 12, 2021. https://www.indiewire.com/features/general/always-jane-review -trans-docuseries-1234678499/.

Luhmann, Niklas. "Frauen, Männer, und George Spencer Brown." *Zeitschrift für Soziologie* 17, no. 1 (1988): 47–71.

Makeham, John. *Name and Actuality in Early Chinese Thought*. Albany: SUNY Press, 1994.

Mao Tse Tung, *Quotations from Mao Tse Tung*. Marxists Internet Archive. https://www.marxists.org/reference/archive/mao/works/red-book/ch31 .htm. 1966.

Marx, Karl. *The German Ideology* (1845). Part 1, "Feuerbach: Opposition of the Materialist and Idealist Outlook." https://www.marxists.org/archive /marx/works/1845/german-ideology/ch01a.htm.

May, Simon. *The Power of Cute*. Princeton, NJ: Princeton University Press, 2019.

McLean, Tui. "The Last of Albania's 'Sworn Virgins.'" BBC News, December 10, 2022. https://www.bbc.com/news/world-europe-63904744.

McLuhan, Marshall, and Quentin Fiore. *The Medium Is the Massage*. London: Penguin, 1967.

Missé, Miquel. *The Myth of the Wrong Body*. Cambridge: Polity Press, 2022.

Moeller, Hans-Georg. "Critique of Eastern Philosophy—Lao Tzu." *Carefree Wandering*. YouTube, 26:00. March 17, 2021. https://www.youtube .com/watch?v=O3y7aiwp4sY.

——. *Dao De Jing*. Chicago: Open Court, 2007.

——. *Daoism Explained: From the Dream of the Butterfly to the Fishnet Allegory*. Chicago: Open Court, 2004.

——. "Daoist Philosophy: Identity | Zhuangzi's The Hunt." YouTube, 12:10. July 7, 2021. *Philosophy in Motion*. https://www.youtube.com/watch?v=wpAKbcPWhgE.

——. "Daoist Philosophy: Right & Wrong | Zhuangzi's Owls and Crows Crave Mice." *Philosophy in Motion*. YouTube, 12:00. April 2024, 2021. https://www.youtube.com/watch?v=yEaPfVCUr2A.

——. "Early Confucian 'Human Supremacy' and Its Daoist Critique." *Asian Studies* 11, no. 3 (2023): 71–92. https://doi.org/10.4312/as.2023.11.3.71-92.

——. "Gangster Zhi: Comedic Daoist Philosophical Practice." *Journal of Chinese Philosophy* 50, no. 1 (2023): 17–27.

——. "Kill Stories: A Critical Narrative in the Zhuangzi." *Dao: A Journal of Comparative Philosophy*, June 29, 2023. https://doi.org/10.1007/s11712-023-09892-w.

——. *The Philosophy of the Daodejing*. New York: Columbia University Press, 2006.

——. "Profilicity: The Definition." *Carefree Wandering*. YouTube, 12:38. February 3, 2025. https://www.youtube.com/watch?v=fk2PpmlxIfA.

——. "Rambling Without Destination: On Daoist You-ing in the World." In *Zhuangzi and the Happy Fish*, edited by Roger T. Ames and Takahiro Nakajima. Honolulu: University of Hawaii Press, 2015.

——. "Zhuangzi's Dream of a Butterfly: A Daoist Interpretation." *Philosophy East and West* 49 (1999).

Moeller, Hans-Georg, and Paul D'Ambrosio. *Genuine Pretending: On the Philosophy of the Zhuangzi*. New York: Columbia University Press, 2017.

——. *You and Your Profile: Identity After Authenticity*. New York: Columbia University Press, 2021.

Moeller, Hans-Georg, Paul D'Ambrosio, Aglaja Strin, and Jorge Ponseti. "Transformation: From (Trans-)Gender Roles to Profiles." *Linacre Quarterly*. 91:3 (2023): 278–95.

Morningstar, Jared. "Trans and Nonbinary Identity in the Age of Profilicity." Medium, October 29, 2021. https://jaredmorningstar.medium.com/trans-and-nonbinary-identity-in-the-age-of-profilicity-65f6162d823c.

Nanda, Serena. *Neither Man nor Woman: The Hijras of India*. Belmont, CA: Wadsworth, 1990.

" 'Nasty Girl' lyrics." AZLyrics. https://www.azlyrics.com/lyrics/eve /nastygirl.html.

New American Bible. https://www.vatican.va/archive/ENG0839/__P4 .HTM.

Nietzsche Source. eKGWB. http://www.nietzschesource.org/

Pang, K. C., et al. "Association of Media Coverage of Transgender and Gender Diverse Issues With Rates of Referral of Transgender Children and Adolescents to Specialist Gender Clinics in the UK and Australia." *JAMA Network Open* 3, no. 7 (2020): https://doi.org/10.1001 /jamanetworkopen.2020.11161.

Plato. *The Republic of Plato.* Translated by Allan Bloom. New York: Basic Books, 1991.

Pletcher, Kenneth. "Consequences of China's One-Child Policy." *Britannica*, February 5, 2025. https://www.britannica.com/topic/one-child -policy/Consequences-of-Chinas-one-child-policy.

Polgreen, Lyida, host. *Ezra Klein Show.* "We Need Better Narratives About Gender." October 10, 2023. YouTube, 1:05:49. https://www.youtube.com /watch?v=h4PVn7_BX0Q.

Ponzetti, James J., ed. *International Encyclopedia of Marriage and Family.* 2nd ed. New York: Macmillan Reference USA, 2003.

Queens. "Nasty Girl." October 1, 2021. YouTube, 3:35. https://www .youtube.com/watch?v=H605IhaMdzM&list=RDH605IhaMdzM &start_radio=1.

"Queens—Season 1." Rotten Tomatoes. https://www.rottentomatoes.com/tv /queens/s01.

Richter, Felix. "Not Married, No Kids." Statista, November 10, 2023. https:// www.statista.com/chart/31238/marriage-and-birth-rate-in-china/.

Rosemont, Henry, Jr. *Against Individualism: A Confucian Rethinking of the Foundations of Morality, Politics, Family, and Religion.* Lanham, MD: Lexington Books, 2015.

Sapolsky, Robert. *Determined: A Science of Life Without Free Will.* New York: Penguin, 2023.

Sartre, Jean-Paul. *No Exit and Three Other Plays.* Translated by Stuart Gilbert. New York: Vintage, 1989.

Sartre, Jean-Paul, Michel Contat, and Michel Rybalka. *Sartre on Theater.* London: Random House, 1976.

Sobotka, Tomás. "World's Highest Childlessness Levels in East Asia." *Population & Societies* 2021/11, no. 595 (2021): 1–4. https://doi.org/10.3917/popsoc.595.0001.

"Solving the Labour Shortage by Arousing the Women to Join in Production" (1955). In *The Socialist Upsurge in China's Countryside*, Chinese ed., vol. 2. Quoted in *Quotations from Mao Tse Tung*, chap. 31. Accessed March 6, 2024. https://www.marxists.org/reference/archive/mao/works/red-book/ch31.htm.

Soong Ching Ling. "Women's Liberation in China." *Peking Review*, no. 6 (February 11, 1972): 6–7. https://www.marxists.org/subject/china/peking-review/1972/PR1972-06a.htm.

Sopelsa, Brooke. "Nearly 30% of Gen Z Women Identify as LGBTQ, Gallup Survey Finds." NBC News, March 13, 2024. https://www.nbcnews.com/news/us-news/nearly-30-gen-z-women-identify-lgbtq-gallup-survey-finds-rcna143019.

——. "NYC Launches Ad Campaign Affirming Trans Bathroom Rights." NBC News, June 7, 2016. https://www.nbcnews.com/feature/nbc-out/nyc-launches-ad-campaign-affirming-trans-bathroom-rights-n586726.

Syed, Renate. "Hijras: India's Third Gender and 2500 Years of Discrimination and Exclusion." Handout presented at "Gender and Violence," Indo-German International Conference, Jawaharlal Nehru University, September 22–24, 2015. https://www.renate-syed.de/artikel/renate-syed-hijras-india-s-third-gender-and-2500-years-of-discrimination-and-exclusion.

Taylor, Charles. *The Ethics of Authenticity*. Cambridge, Mass.: Harvard University Press, 1992.

——. *A Secular Age*. Cambridge, Mass.: Harvard University Press, 2007.

Textor, C. "Urban and Rural Population of China from 2014 to 2024." Statista, January 17, 2025. https://www.statista.com/statistics/278566/urban-and-rural-population-of-china/.

Tracy, Jessica L., and Richard W. Robins. "Putting the Self Into Self-Conscious Emotions: A Theoretical Model." *Psychological Inquiry* 15, no. 2 (April 2004): 103–25. https://doi.org/10.1207/s15327965pli1502_01.

"Trans-Gesetz: Wissen sie, was sie tun?" *Emma*, October 25, 2023. https://www.emma.de/artikel/wissen-sie-was-sie-tun-340653.

Trilling, Lionel. *Sincerity and Authenticity*. Cambridge, MA: Harvard University Press, 1972.

Tu, Irene. "Big 'They' Energy." *Stand Up Comedy*. October 12, 2023. You-Tube, 10:47. https://www.youtube.com/watch?v=GKcUe-LbYSY.

Walker, Esther. "Top Cat: How 'Hello Kitty' Conquered the World." *Independent*, May 21, 2008. https://www.independent.co.uk/news/world/asia/top-cat-how-hello-kitty-conquered-the-world-831522.html.

Wang Ping. *Aching for Beauty*. New York: Knopf Doubleday, 2002.

Wang, Robin R. *Yinyang: The World of Heaven and Earth in Chinese Thought and Culture*. New York: Cambridge University Press, 2012.

Whiteman, Hilary. "Ballerina's Parents Jailed for Neglecting the Daughter They Bathed in Attention but Starved of Food." CNN, February 15, 2025. https://edition.cnn.com/2025/02/15/australia/australia-malnourished-girl-neglect-hnk-intl/index.html.

Wikipedia. "Always Jane." https://en.wikipedia.org/wiki/Always_Jane.

——. "Hello Kitty." https://en.wikipedia.org/wiki/Hello_Kitty.

——. "List of Gender Identities." https://en.wikipedia.org/wiki/List_of_gender_identities

——. "Rapid-onset gender dysphoria controversy." https://en.wikipedia.org/wiki/Rapid-onset_gender_dysphoria_controversy#cite_note-hrc-35

——. "Three Obediences and Four Virtues." https://en.wikipedia.org/wiki/Three_Obediences_and_Four_Virtues.

——. "*Queens* (American TV series)," https://en.wikipedia.org/wiki/Queens_(American_TV_series)

Wynn, Natalie. "Autogynephilia." *ContraPoints*. February 2, 2018. YouTube, 48:54. https://www.youtube.com/watch?v=6czRFLs5JQo.

——. "Gender Critical." *ContraPoints*. March 31, 2019. YouTube, 33:48. https://www.youtube.com/watch?v=1pTPuoGjQsI&t=500s.

——. "J. K. Rowling." *ContraPoints*. January 26, 2021. YouTube, 1:29:44. https://www.youtube.com/watch?v=7gDKbT_l2us&t=1691s.

——. "Pronouns." *ContraPoints*. November 3, 2018. YouTube, 31:55. https://www.youtube.com/watch?v=9bbINLWtMKI&t=1622s.

——. "'Transtrenders.'" *ContraPoints*. July 2, 2019. YouTube, 34:43. https://www.youtube.com/watch?v=EdvM_pRfuFM&t=1480s.

——. "Twilight." *ContraPoints*. March 2, 2024. YouTube, 2:52:26. https://www.youtube.com/watch?v=bqloPw5wp48.

Yurcaba, Jo. "'Social Contagion' Isn't Causing More Youths to Be Transgender, Study Finds." NBC News, August 4, 2022. https://www.nbcnews

.com/nbc-out/out-health-and-wellness/social-contagion-isnt-causing
-youths-transgender-study-finds-rcna41392.

Zapata, Jamie. "Transgender Day of Remembrance Is a Time for Authenticity." *Inman*, November 18, 2023. https://www.inman.com/2023/11/18
/transgender-day-of-remembrance-is-a-time-for-authenticity/.

Zhen Tian. "Freedom Cannot Be Given: An Analysis of the Significance of
Women in the Cultural Revolution." *The UC Santa Barbara Undergraduate Journal of History* (Fall 2021). Accessed March 7, 2024. https://
undergradjournal.history.ucsb.edu/our-journal/past-issues/fall-2021/tian/.

Ziporyn, Brook, trans. *Zhuangzi: The Complete Writings*. Indianapolis:
Hackett, 2020.

INDEX

GPSR Authorized Representative: Easy Access System Europe, Mustamäe tee
50, 10621 Tallinn, Estonia, gpsr.requests@easproject.com